THE
LOST KINGDOM

Memoir of an Afghan Prince

H. R. H. PRINCE ALI SERAJ OF AFGHANISTAN

A POST HILL PRESS BOOK
ISBN: 978-1-68261-518-8
ISBN (eBook): 978-1-68261-519-5

Cover art by Christian Bentulan

Some names and locations have been changed to protect the privacy of individuals

Post Hill Press
New York • Nashville
posthillpress.com

Published in the United States of America

DEDICATION

This book is dedicated to my three beautiful daughters, Princess Sahar Alexandra, Princess Safia Emerett, and Princess Alia Elizabeth, without whom I would feel incomplete and my work would have been a waste.

It is because of the love and support my family so generously dispensed that I felt compelled to put ink to paper and speak my Afghanistan back to my life.

I remember a time away from the clamors of war and clashes of weapons. I remember the dreams my forefathers held for this land of ours, this people . . . Afghanistan is more to me than a land-locked nation in the heart of Central Asia.

My Afghanistan still echoes of happiness and breathtaking beauty. Those are the memories I want to conjure so that you may learn of my people and see how their progressive and prosperous future was interrupted.

Afghanistan has suffered many great injustices, and as its prince I owe my nation the courtesy of its history. Afghanistan's story deserves to be told from a place of courage and dignity, for Afghans are a deserving people.

Afghans are a resilient people, a capable people, a good people. Greed and illegitimate ambitions destroyed my nation and stole its future.

Here, in the pages that follow, I will safeguard Afghanistan memory and restore my nation's sovereign right and integrity away from terror, radicalism, and covert imperialism.

I dedicate this book to my loved ones, to my children and grandchildren. Know that I am proud of all of you and of all your choices and accomplishments. May you find in my words a newfound strength; may you remember that Afghanistan will always be your birth right to keep, but never to own. Royalty, I have learned, is not a statement of ownership over a land, but rather an oath to safeguard a people and a land from nefarious forces. To that end, I have held true to the best of my ability.

My loyalty forever remains tied to Afghanistan and all Afghans, beyond creed and ethnicity. My lineage is an old one—since 867 AD my forefathers have watched over Afghanistan and its future. I pray that my book will serve a testament to their memories, their deeds, and their hopes.

Long after I am gone I pray that my book will endure and speak of the land that captured my heart and breathed strength in my soul. Afghanistan will forever remain my home, my beloved, my own.

May Allah All Mighty (SWT) look upon us all with mercy.

TABLE OF CONTENTS

INTRODUCTION

A ROYAL LEGACY

F ollowing is the story of my life, or rather the love affair I have enjoyed with Afghanistan, the land of my forefathers, my first and last love, my anchor and my strength.

A prince of Afghanistan, I have lived most of my life in exile, forced to run before the violence of the Soviet Union, forced to stay away before the radicalism of the Taliban, and forced to watch as my nation went up in flames, eaten whole by the greed of men.

An Afghan prince educated in the West, I have lived my life in between two worlds, my heart tethered by my two great loves: Afghanistan and my American wife.

This book covers 30 years of my life (1978 to 2014), from the fall of the monarchy to communism and the rise of the Taliban and the subsequent coming of Osama bin Laden to the US and NATO invasion of Afghanistan following the 9/11 terror attacks.

You will learn of Afghanistan through my eyes, and maybe learn along the way that history bears many witnesses, each to their memory, each to their own subjective recollection.

I make claim to no truth but my own.

My tale is that of an Afghan prince who for decades on end has witnessed the disappearing of his heritage to the fires of war and despair. I have long dedicated my life work to righting the many wrongs that have befallen my homeland and will continue to offer my life to my people so that their voices can be heard. Afghanistan's story needs to be told.

I am the direct descendant of nine generations of kings of Afghanistan: the nephew of His Majesty King Amanullah (reigned from 1919-1929), known as the Victor of Afghanistan; the grandson of His Majesty Amir Habibullah (reigned 1901-1919); and the great-grandson of His Majesty Amir Abdurrahman (reigned 1880-1901), known as the "Iron King." My ancestry continues on to His Majesty Amir Dost Mohammad, who assumed the throne in1827. My entire family line can be traced back to 867 AD. In many ways, my family has been Afghanistan's keeper, its memory, its traditions, and its national integrity.

I was born in Kabul, Afghanistan, the middle child with an elder brother, Abdullah, and younger sister, Salma. Our father, Prince Abdul Ghafoor, was one of the younger sons of His Majesty Amir Habibullah who, besides attending to the affairs of the country as monarch, also enjoyed hunting and photography on big-game expeditions through Afghanistan and India. This king, my grandfather, had 36 wives, to whom he sired 29 sons and 32 daughters. Marriages back then guaranteed tribal stability and allegiance. Kings married often to ensure order and tribal cooperation, not to pursue carnal desires.

My family was big, eclectic in its personalities—a reflection of Afghanistan's ethnic make-up and testament to our nation's diversity and wealth. We were all Afghanistan's sons and daughters, proud of our heritage and lineage . . . Afghanistan has run in my veins since long before I drew my first breath. It is likely my last breath will be spent speaking its name.

We were our people! For generations of men, Afghans have looked upon our house and recognized their own kin. Such was the strength of my house and such has been our legacy.

Back when my great-grandfather assumed the monarchy in 1880, Afghanistan was a puzzle of principalities devoid of real unity. Amir Abdurrahman Khan, also known as the Iron King, or more simply as Amir, changed that political reality.

To keep the tribes of Afghanistan together and prevent sedition following his grand unification campaign, my grandfather picked a wife from among each tribe. I realize that Afghanistan's tribal system may sound archaic, even medieval to Westerners, so I ask you to understand one crucial point.

What the West calls multiculturalism, Afghanistan calls tribalism. Our many colors, traditions, cultures, sensitivities, and strengths are carried, expressed, and encapsulated within our tribal system. More importantly, it is through the tribes that Afghans have together secured and exercised their rights to political determination. Afghanistan's true tribalism, that of which my family stood a keeper and represented, was not a euphemism for feudalism, but an affirmation of Afghan's civil rights.

Afghanistan was born on the back of the tribes, and it is the tribes that have kept Afghanistan's integrity safe. I believe the tribes will save Afghanistan from those radical hordes that have held my people hostage.

Misconceptions by many in the West have clouded their thoughts and tainted their views of my homeland. Afghanistan is not a devilish black hole of barbarism. Afghanistan is a land occupied by barbarous legions; it is a land violated, a people tortured, a culture hijacked.

On these pages, I reclaim what was stolen from us. Afghanistan is more than a few borders drawn on a map. Afghanistan is a hope captured on the lips of our children. It is the sun setting on our mountains, the breath in our lungs, and the song in our hearts. Afghanistan has not sung its last—legitimacy is still here, the tribes are still here, and our people are indeed willing.

////////////

After King Habibullah Khan, the martyred king, was brought back to Kabul to be buried, my uncle, His Majesty King Amanullah, the Amir's second eldest son, rose to power after his brother, Prince Enayatullah, refused the throne. Upon ascension, King Amanullah's first act as monarch was to declare a war of independence against the British. The empire would soon learn of Afghanistan's independence.

A united body, the tribes rallied around my uncle, unbending and proud. If Afghanistan had allowed once for its borders to be breached, its sons and daughters fought bravely to reclaim their land away from the foreign invader. This was to be the last of three Anglo-Afghan wars (1832 to 1842, 1879, and 1920). Independence was to be Afghanistan's victory march. I pray that soon it will be so again. Today Afghanistan is up against a tyrant much more pernicious and cruel. Bravery and sacrifice will be needed to expel those forces that have polluted my land and held my people captive.

Afghanistan once echoed of laughter, hope, and brilliant tomorrows. The Afghanistan I remember was a land of plenty, of breathtaking beauty.

King Amanullah ushered in a new era, not only in Afghanistan, but also in India and as far away as Egypt. In fact, he is fondly mentioned both in Mahatma Gandhi's and Gamal Abdel Nasser's memoirs. In 1924, the king introduced Afghanistan's first constitution and parliament, built hospitals and additional schools, freed the slaves, and brought in railroads and factories. The first airplanes were brought in from Italy. He freed Afghan women from the veil by abolishing it, and sent the first group of Afghan girls to study medicine in Turkey. He also sent male and female students to France and Germany so they could benefit from Western culture and bring modernism to Afghanistan.

My uncle's goals were to open up Afghanistan to the rest of the world and reform our entire national structure by strengthening state institutions.

In the ten years of my uncle's rule, Afghanistan was firmly set onto the road to economic development. Part of that was related to his very close and friendly working relationship with Ataturk of Turkey.

For as far as memory stretches, my family, my line has worked to transform Afghanistan into a modern state, maybe not that which Western powers envisioned, but a modern nation, nevertheless.

But our future was interrupted. The blame lies at the door of those who betrayed, plotted, and schemed covert imperialism.

////////

Where did Afghanistan go wrong? This is a question I often ask myself. At which point in our history did we lose to hatred and radicalism? In my view, Afghanistan was sold out to radicalism. My homeland was invaded and held hostage from 1978 to 2001, first by communism, then by Al Qaeda and the Taliban, followed by the barbarism called Wahhabism. While communism was forced upon us by the Soviet Union and their Afghan underlings, Al Qaeda and Wahhabism have been a poison forced upon us by powers whose ambition has been to wield control through socio-political annihilation.

Afghanistan has been wrongly associated with terrorism. Afghans are not by definition radical; rather, they are being held captive by the theo-political construct of Wahhabism, the ideology that Saudi Arabia, Qatar, and other Islamic powers use to anchor their dominions.

I argue that my homeland was set on the path to political perdition by the British Empire in the 1920s, when bigotry was exploited to score political points. At that time, King Amanulla's wife, Queen Soraya, stood as a powerful influence on Central Asia. A progressive woman, Queen Soraya was a champion for women's rights and a strong supporter of progress. My mother, Lady Siddiqa, was Queen Soraya's first cousin.

Keen to avenge the black mark Afghanistan left on its military legacy, Britain devised a plan that would eventually bring Afghans to their knees and set in motion nefarious dynamics.

While King Amanullah was concentrating on developing his nation, the British were planning his downfall. During King Amanullah's European tour to introduce Afghanistan to the Western world, he was greeted with fanfare in England. Colorful banners hung on the reception route to welcome him as he rode with King George V. Queen Soraya accompanied Queen Mary in the carriages that weaved their way through the throngs of well-wishers. A now-famous photo of Queen Soraya, dressed in a beautiful sleeveless dress and diamond tiara, appeared in all the British newspapers.

It was this photo that the British used against King Amanullah in 1929 to instigate a revolution under the leadership of a highway thief by the name of Kalakani. He was allegedly paid 50,000 Pounds Sterling to initiate the revolution by labelling the king an infidel. Under the Crown's command, spies such as Mullah e Lang ("the lame mullah"), dressed as holy men, infiltrated Central Asia through India where they distributed copies of the queen's sleeveless photo as proof of her said heresy. Several pictures were subsequently doctored to underscore the alleged salacious nature of the Afghan monarchy to inflame religious passions and fuel an uprising.

From the ashes of Afghanistan's fallen monarchy, the empire aspired to assert control and finally claim ownership over Central

Asia against their colonial contenders. Perfectly in tune, two tribes, the Shinwaris and the Momands, rose against King Amanullah.

Eager to protect his people from another bloodbath and refusing to have one drop of Afghan blood spilled on his behalf, the king abdicated. Broken-hearted, he went into exile to Italy upon the invitation of King Victor Emmanuelle III.

The rebels ruled for nine months. In late 1929, General Nadir Shah, a cousin and the minister of defense during the reign of King Amanullah, together with his four brothers, returned to Afghanistan to wage a war of restoration against Kalakani and to pave the way for the return of the king.

While Kalakani was defeated, King Amanullah never returned to Afghanistan, thus passing the throne to Nadir Shah. Our line remained unbroken until April 26, 1978, when Soviet-backed Afghan communist parties, and again in December 25, 1979, communist Russia laid a claim against our homeland, sealing in one smooth swoop the destiny of an entire people.

Never since has Afghanistan tasted peace. Never since has spring graced our skies . . . only winter.

///////////

I am a son of Afghanistan. I was born and raised within a monarchical culture that perceived itself not a reigning house over a submissive nation, but the keeper of a tradition entrusted with the momentous task of forging a future worthy of our people's aspirations. Afghanistan may have been a monarchy, but it was never a tyranny. Our monarchy was based on our ancestral system of popular representation and multi-culturalism.

A prince of Afghanistan, my education was both Western and Afghan. Following King Amanullah's, and thereafter the family's, emphasis on learning, I finished my primary education at the French academy, Lycée Isteqlal, in Kabul. When my father was assigned to the Afghan Embassy in Karachi, Pakistan, I transferred to Saint Patrick's High School in that city. While in Karachi, I had the opportunity to meet and mingle with boys and girls from different nations. I fell in love with a young American girl and developed a liking for American culture—America would remain one of my great loves, a home away from my own.

When we returned from Pakistan I completed my schooling at the Afghan Institute of Technology. After graduation, I was sent to Helmand Valley to work on the Grishk power plant, a joint Afghan-American project. I had the opportunity to go abroad for college, and since my education in Pakistan was in English I was given the choice of England or the United States. With my historical dislike of the British, I opted for the United States and attended the University of Connecticut, where I studied agricultural economics and business.

After graduation from the university I returned to Afghanistan and established several successful businesses, including a travel agency, a taxi service (a precursor of Uber), advertising and employment agencies, and world-famous restaurants that served guests such as Japan's Crown Prince Akihito (presently the emperor) and his wife, writer Leon Uris, French author Joseph Kassel, French designer Pierre Balmain, and other celebrities. My restaurants were the places to be and be seen for Kabul's cosmopolitan elites, aristocrats, embassy crowd, visiting dignitaries, and international intelligence operatives playing spy vs. spy. In addition to my entrepreneurial ventures I was very actively involved in my countrymen's welfare. I assisted the poor by setting them up in private business so they could stop begging on the streets.

In 1974, I married the love of my life, a beautiful Irish-American girl, Maribeth Cecilia Blawie, whom I had met and fallen in love with after graduating from the University of Connecticut. We settled in Kabul, where over the next five years she bore me two lovely girls. Our dreams and plans were shattered in 1978 when I was put on the list of those to be executed by the new communist regime. As a member of the ruling family and well connected to foreign diplomats and international businesses, I was a threat to the communist establishment. Realizing that our lives were in jeopardy, I consulted with Adolph Dubs, the newly appointed United States Ambassador to Afghanistan, and with the assistance of my trusted bodyguard devised an elaborate scheme to escape from Afghanistan.

This is when my story truly began . . .

Disguised as a hippie, with my wife and young daughters in tow, we embarked on a perilous bus ride to Pakistan via the Khyber Pass and multiple communist checkpoints.

Settling in my wife's home state of Connecticut, I was considered nothing more than a refugee from a faraway communist country. Once the *enfant terrible* of one of the oldest royal families of the East, I struggled with this new reality and identity. But my optimism and entrepreneurial spirit would help me find success over the course of the next twenty-three years.

During the dark days of the Afghan jihad against the Soviet Red Army, I led activities and programs to help my people by providing food and clothing through charitable organizations. I worked tirelessly for the benefit of Afghanistan's freedom fighters by giving public speeches and meeting with members of the U.S. Congress. Working closely with the Reagan administration to help defeat the Soviet invaders in Afghanistan, I was instrumental in getting Soviet-made armaments and American Stinger missiles to the Afghan freedom fighters. I also assisted other Afghans who had escaped the scourge of the communists and Al Qaeda settle in the United States.

More than two decades after leaving Afghanistan I returned to a nation that had been destroyed from years of war, Taliban rule, and months of U.S. aerial bombardment. The country was a shadow of what it once was. Despite the misgivings of many of my friends and family, I began to spend most of my time in Afghanistan, determined to help the country rebuild. I constructed more than three hundred homes, several mosques for the poor in various provinces, and supplied school materials for thousands of students.

This work, coupled by the Afghan tribes' overwhelming support of my family, helped me develop a very important relationship with all the tribes. To utilize this relationship for the strength of the country, and at the behest of the tribal elders, I created the National Coalition for Dialogue with the Tribes of Afghanistan (NCDTA).

I believed that only by uniting the tribes and empowering the people could we begin to address and solve the enormous socio-political-economic problems facing the nation, the growing distance between the central government and the people, the resurgence of Al Qaeda/ Taliban forces, and the ensuing death and destruction of my people and country. Forming the NDCTA was the first step in my mission to officially unify the tribes and help save our faltering democracy.

My decision to invest decades of my time and energy in Afghanistan came at a price. It took a devastating toll on my marriage, my emotional and spiritual well-being, and my health. But I continue this work today, and the history and events that unfold in these pages are a testament both to my family's legacy and the resilience and courage of the Afghan people. My one goal and hope remains the same, that one day the legacy of my royal lineage—a peaceful and prosperous Afghanistan—will once again be restored.

CHAPTER 1

COMMUNISTS AT THE DOOR

KABUL, APRIL 26, 1978

It was a grey morning. Dark clouds were hanging over the city. Far off a dust storm was brewing and I felt a certain gnawing in the pit of stomach. As a child I could always feel when something bad was about to happen. I had inherited this trait from my mother and others on her side of the family.

As teenagers growing up in Karachi, Pakistan, my brother always depended on my sixth sense to know whether or not we were going to get into trouble when we did something that our parents were unaware of, like sneaking out of our house in the middle of the night to visit girlfriends or go to a party. My instincts proved right nearly 100 percent of the time, and now the feeling was stronger than ever.

This was the morning that President Daoud Khan, a distant cousin of mine, had convened a cabinet meeting at the presidential palace to decide the fate of the communist leaders whom he had ordered to be arrested a few days earlier. A man named Nur Mohammad Taraki headed the communist party at that time. His deputy, Hafizullah Amin, had escaped arrest. President Daoud had been digging his own grave by trying to maneuver the country away from the Soviet sphere of influence. His efforts to establish closer relations with Western and moderate Islamic countries aroused the suspicions of the Soviet Union, which began to lend an increasing degree of support to its communist protégés in Afghanistan. He had made a trip to the Middle East to wean Afghanistan away from Soviet authority, and Arab leaders told him they would provide financial support if he got rid of the communist party in Afghanistan. Upon his return from the Middle East, he passed a decree to arrest all communist leaders.

I observed these events as a resident of Kabul, a member of the royal family, and the owner of a popular supper club, The Golden Lotus, where throngs of Iranian students had sung, until recently, the praises of President Daoud. The situation in neighboring Iran was deteriorating in 1978, and before his change of heart about communism and the Soviets, Daoud had won the admiration of those Iranian students who were members of the communist Todeh party. Over Chinese food and rounds of drinks they told stories about Daoud's coup d'état against his first cousin, King Mohammad Zahir Shah, whom he dethroned with the help of the communist party members of Afghanistan in 1973. And they discussed the imminent downfall of the Shah of Iran, Reza Shah Pahlawi.

President Daoud's latest actions, however, were costing him those admiring communist fans. On April 17, 1978, a member of the communist People's Democratic Party of Afghanistan (PDPA) and critic of the president was killed. His funeral turned into an anti-government rally, which led Daoud to arrest the PDPA leaders, including Taraki, several days later.

The night before the cabinet meeting, Amin, one of the PDPA leaders who had escaped arrest, had allegedly contacted party members within the tank division and air force at the Puli Charkhi military camp, about 10 kilometers from the capitol, alerting them to be ready.

On that morning of the cabinet meeting, Kabul University students were planning to march toward the presidential palace to air their grievances.

The Minister of Defense, General Rasoul, was informed of the students' plans and asked to deploy the Puli Charkhi tank division to guard the palace. He granted the request and summoned the tanks, unaware that the request was a ploy by Amin and his associates in the camp.

Around 10:00 a.m. that fateful morning, while I was having breakfast outside on the porch of my house, I heard muffled cannon fire coming from the direction of the palace. Having served in the tank division, I immediately recognized the sound of those blasts.

At the same time, my aide, Jan Ali, a young Hazara man and the son of a tribal chieftain, informed me that my brother Abdullah was on the phone. Abdullah was my older brother and partner in my business ventures, including the Golden Lotus. As soon as I picked up the receiver, I heard the worry in my brother's voice as he asked me to come to the restaurant. The Golden Lotus was located around the corner from the presidential palace, which also housed President Daoud's residence.

Taking a quick shower and combing my goatee, which I had grown since my days of working for the Afghan government in Helmand Valley in the 1960s, I got dressed and headed for the garage. Jan Ali, who was never more than 10 feet away from me, followed close on my heels. Before I got to the garage, I told my "Man Friday" to protect my wife and children by keeping all the gates closed and not letting anyone in. He smiled and, opening his jacket to expose the pistol that he had tucked away in his belt, told me not to worry. He said he would guard the *Khanum Sahib* (a title given to all foreign ladies) with his life. I did not doubt his allegiance to my family or me for a moment.

Getting into my Jaguar Mark X, I made my way through the streets to the Blue Mosque intersection, which led to the restaurant and the palace. At the intersection, a bewildered traffic policeman stopped me. He recognized me and politely advised me to take the back street, as he had heard that there was trouble down the road where I was headed.

Taking his advice, I swerved my car to the left and made my way toward Butcher Street, so named because of the number of butcher shops occupying both sides of this narrow street. Every morning the butchers would bring the live animals to their shops and slaughter them right there on the sidewalk, allowing the blood to flow in the open *juis* (ditches) that ran along both sides of the streets of Kabul.

Arriving at the restaurant, I parked the car along the row of fountains near the Japanese garden that led to the restaurant. I saw my brother and all the employees standing on the sidewalk, looking towards the Lotus Intersection at the residence of Prince Naim, brother of President Daoud. I looked in that direction, but could not see anything through the heavy dust that was gusting at the time. Finally, peering through the dust, I noticed soldiers in full battle gear lying in the ditch.

They were all pointing their Kalashnikovs in the direction of the president's residence. The sound of the tank cannons was getting more steady and rapid. I realized then that the palace may be under attack, and later learned that my assumption was right. The very tanks that had arrived under the pretense of protecting the palace from the onslaught of the students had in fact attacked the palace. During the bloody fight between the tanks and the 2,500 palace guards, every guard was killed while defending the palace and the president.

During its history, this was the second time that the palace had come under attack (the first attack was in 1929). The palace was built on an 80-acre site in the center of the capitol during the reign of my great-grandfather Amir Abdurrahman Khan in the 1800s, with his own money. My father was born and lived in the palace until the age of sixteen. Three fortified walls of solid stones, with the outer wall reaching 20 to 30 meters in height, protect the palace compound. The main gate, which stands about 10 meters high, is made of thick, solid oak.

The 2,500 palace guards have traditionally been posted on the outer wall, and inside the main gate stands a second stone wall surrounding the grounds of the inner palace. A division of T62 Russian tanks is parked in the space between those walls to further protect the president.

Beyond these walls are gardens made up of green lawns and fields of roses and every other flower imaginable. The inner buildings are divided into several sections. One section, called the Haram Sarai, was built to house the king's wives and the princes and princesses during my grandfather's reign. The garden within this section contains two enormous white birch trees that were planted by my great-grandfather Amir Abdurrahman himself. The trunks of those trees are now more than ten meters in diameter. In another part of this section the king, and later the president, presided over meetings and greeted all visitors. Next to the Haram Sarai is a small, Mogul-style palace called Kot-e Baghcha. This was the personal residence of Amir Abdurrahman Khan. The entire inner walls were covered with colorful miniature drawings in the Mogul Empire style.

While we were watching the soldiers and their Russian machine guns and wondering what was going on, my cousin Abdul Kabir and his son Zia arrived at the restaurant, totally bewildered. We all stood there for a while, each trying to decide what to do, and I finally broke the silence to say that I had to get back to my house. My American-born wife Beth and our daughters Sahar, who was two-and-a-half at the time, and little Safia, who was six months old, were alone.

Abdul Kabir asked me to give him a ride home, as he lived not far from me. When we got near his house, he asked me to drop him off on the corner of Sher-e-Now Park so he could buy cigarettes. As I was driving toward the park I heard the screaming of MIG jets zigzagging in the skies above, followed by the sound of helicopters.

As I dropped Abdul Kabir off on the corner and turned left toward the Blue Mosque intersection, I saw a MIG bear down on the street where I had dropped off my cousin. Soon thereafter I heard machine gun fire. I later found out that a burst of the bullets had killed a number of pedestrians and also made a gaping hole in Abdul Kabir's upper thigh. Apparently, seeing the jet coming, he had jumped inside a *jui* by the park. The ditch was deep enough to protect his body, but his thigh was left exposed. Saved by the *jui*, he was taken to the army hospital, where a Russian doctor operated on him.

When I arrived home, Jan Ali greeted me at the garage door. I walked toward the house, down the long cobblestone walkway covered by grape vines hanging overhead, and followed by my two retrievers and a German Shepherd named Khan.

As I was explaining the situation to Beth, who had just returned to Kabul from the States after giving birth to Safia, I heard the whirring roar of a helicopter. I walked out to see what was going on. Little Sahar was playing in the garden with the maid. I looked up at the military fort located on the hill behind our house as the helicopter suddenly zoomed toward the fort and opened fire with rockets. The sounds of rocket and gunfire echoed so loudly that Sahar ran screaming into the arms of her maid. (For a long time thereafter, even when she was in the United States, Sahar would run and hide whenever she spotted a helicopter.)

The soldiers from the fort opened fire on the helicopter and over our house onto the street. All hell broke loose. The skies over Kabul were filled with screaming MIGs and helicopters. The rattle of gunfire and booms of falling bombs echoed throughout the Kabul Valley. The house shook and the windows clattered. Khan was so nervous that he tore the house's screen door off its hinges and ran and hid under our bed.

I picked up the phone and called the deputy ambassador at the American embassy to find out what we should do. When he answered the phone, he sounded very nervous and his voice sounded like it was coming from the bottom of a barrel. He told me that he was hiding under the table as there were bullets whizzing by the embassy.

He advised me to stay indoors and added that if things got dangerous I should call him again, and he would send an escort vehicle to deliver Beth and the kids to the embassy.

That was my last conversation with him. Soon thereafter our phones went dead.

I became concerned about my father who lived across the street from our house, so I ran over to check on him. My mother and sister were out of the country at the time. I found him sitting calmly in the living room, busily occupied with his favorite pastime . . . writing poetry. As a young man he had experienced similar chaos in 1929, when the family was besieged in the palace during the British-instigated uprising of Bachai Saqau, a rebel and highway thief financed and supported by the British to dethrone my uncle H.M. King Amanullah. My father was 16 years old during that attack.

I asked him to join us in our house for lunch. When we returned to my house I turned on the radio to get the news, but found only martial music on all channels. This proved but one thing: the radio station had fallen into the hands of those who had instigated the takeover.

The bombardment kept on all afternoon. My brother-in-law Tamim Etemadi, son of the former Prime Minister Noor Ahmad Etemadi, who was now the Afghan Ambassador to Pakistan, lived in an apartment close to the palace. I called him to check on how was doing since his wife, my sister Salma, was also abroad with my mother. It took some time for him to answer the phone. He spoke in a muffled tone. He told me that a bomb had exploded near his apartment and the shrapnel had smashed through the windows and ripped the inside walls. I asked him to come to our house immediately, which he did. Around evening things got a bit quiet, but still no news as to who or what was in charge. All night the air reverberated with the sound of distant gunfire.

Unbeknownst to us at the time, President Daoud had gathered as many of his family members as he could inside a room called

Gulkhana, or flower room, in the palace. During the ensuing gunfire his eldest son, Omar, was struck with shrapnel from an exploding bomb outside the window where he was standing. While he lay dying in his mother's lap, one of Daoud's twin sons, fearing what would become of his wife and kids if they fell into the hands of the communists, opened fire with the Kalashnikov he was holding, killing his wife, children, and himself. Just then a group of soldiers belonging to the communist party burst into the room and opened fire. During the barrage of gunfire, President Daoud, his brother Naim, Daoud's other son, their wives and other family members were massacred, some 19 members in all, including several toddlers.

The next morning, the usual martial music on the radio was suddenly interrupted by an announcement that President Daoud was dead and the country was now in the hands of the Khalq Party (Communist People's Party), headed by Taraki. Overnight, life as we knew it came to an abrupt and bloody end. Our family's era of ruling Afghanistan was over.

CHAPTER 2

THE END OF THE WORLD

This sudden turn of events in Afghanistan's history concerned me a great deal. We were going through uncharted waters, and as an Afghan Prince I felt deep fear for the country and my immediate family for the first time. Since our family had ruled Afghanistan for over two hundred years, I was reminded of what happened to the family of Czar Nicholas of Russia after the Bolshevik revolution and feared the same fate—or worse—for us.

The new regime, dominated by Nur Mohammad Taraki's Khalqi communist party, argued that their leading role in the "revolution" made them the natural ruling party. They backed up this claim with Brezhnev-like rhetoric about world peace, replete with invocations of the masses and the internationalist character of their revolution. This self-serving argument was used to legitimate the marginalization of the Parcham communist party, which claimed that without the participation of its officers, victory would never have been achieved.

The Khalqi regime believed that it was their right to monopolize power; they rejected any coalition with existing political parties and denied them their right to carry out political activities. They declared five groups as enemies: the Parchamis, Islamists, Maoists, Setam-i Melli (itself divided into the factions of Badakhshi and Bahes), and Afghan Mellat.

These groups were not the only ones deemed to be enemies of the regime. The intelligentsia, political figures from previous regimes, local notables, and religious leaders all became the target of repression. The elimination of "enemies" was justified as a necessary step for the protection of the people and the success of the revolution. Noor Mohammad Taraki himself declared war against "bearded men," i.e. the clergy. In a televised speech, he instructed the Khalqis that "those who plot against us in darkness must be eliminated in darkness."

As such, many members of the ancient regime and Daoud Khan loyalists were taken from their homes and held in the basement of the Ministry of Defense before being transferred to the dreaded Pul-e-Charkhi prison on the outskirts of Kabul.

We could not do anything but wait to see what fate had in store for us. That afternoon, a few hours after learning about President Daoud's death on the radio, I was having high tea on the terrace when my cousin Obaidullah Tarzi arrived and filled me in on what was going on. He told me about the multitudes of civilians who had been killed. He talked about the bodies lying around the Palace and the body parts stuck on tree branches. I left the table—I could not bear to hear any more.

My cousin asked me if I had a passport, because one of his friends had obtained the seal of the Khalq party and could certify my passport with it, which would make it easier for me to leave the country if I chose. Putting this seal on my passport would cost 30,000 afghanis, or about $600. I gave him the money and my passport and he promised to return before the 7:00 p.m. curfew. He returned with my newly stamped passport at about 6:30, and then quickly left. I continued to think things through.

I looked across the yard at the swing set that the carpenters had set up for Sahar. Strange thoughts began swirling through my head. I walked over to the swings and stood under the top beam. It was taller than I was. I realized that if the communists came for me, they may hang me from that beam, and I did not want Sahar to see her father hanging from her swing set. I called Jan Ali and told him to have a carpenter cut the height down to below my chin. Satisfied with my decision, I walked over to the terrace and sat down in a chair facing the swing set. Beth was inside reading a bedtime story to Sahar, who was still very edgy about the day's happenings and the helicopters.

As I sat and wondered about our next steps, I could hear Beth humming a song to Sahar. Little Safia was already asleep. Hearing her sweet and gentle voice, my mind drifted to the time I first met this beautiful Irish-American girl.

In the autumn of 1969 I had just graduated from the University of Connecticut. While at the university I had met a young woman named Pamela Blawie, who came from a very wealthy family from Fairfield, Connecticut. Her father was a prominent lawyer in Fairfield County, and her mother, judging from the photographs Pam showed me, was a beautiful, redheaded Irish-American, a real lady. Pamela also graduated that year, and she invited me to her graduation party at her family's home.

When I walked into the Blawie mansion with my roommate, Jeff Tunick, I noticed a beautiful, long-legged, bikini-clad beauty sitting on a chair by the pool, surrounded by a group of guys. They were each trying to impress her anyway they could, but she was not paying attention to anyone in particular.

I asked Pam who the long-haired beauty was, and she told me that she was her younger sister. They were going to be leaving soon for a trip to Ireland together. I did not even know the girl's name, but it was love at first sight and at that moment I decided that she was going to be my wife. To make sure that I would see her again, I approached Pam and suggested that since they were going to go to Ireland via London, she should contact my sister Salma, who was at that time studying in London. I gave Pam Salma's phone number and left without meeting her sister, whose name, I learned later, was Maribeth.

When I told Jeff about my plans, he laughed and told me that I had made a great choice. He knew a few things about Maribeth's background, such as her choice to work at a gas station instead of a cushy office after graduating from the preppy girls' school, Manhattanville College. She later worked as a waitress in a Chinese restaurant in New Haven, Connecticut, where she was so well liked that Peter Chang, the owner/chef, named one of his dishes after her, calling it "Maribeth Meatless," because she was a vegetarian at the time.

Jeff went on to describe Beth as a real hippy and flower child; it was well known that she had participated in anti-Vietnam war demonstrations in Washington, DC, and placed flowers in the barrels of the soldiers' guns as they stood guarding the Capitol Building. The more he talked, the more intrigued I became with this fascinating woman.

That evening I called Salma and told her that two sisters were coming to London and they would contact her. I told her that even though I had not even been introduced to her yet, I was going to marry the younger of the two. Being my younger sister and a good friend, Salma did not argue the point. She agreed to meet them.

The sisters came back from Ireland a week before I moved back to Afghanistan, and one day Pam called me and invited me to her parents' twenty-fifth wedding anniversary. As we drove to Fairfield, she told me about her trip and meeting my sister in London. By time we got to her house, many of the guests were already there, gathered around the swimming pool. The theme for the evening was Hawaiian and all the girls were dressed in grass skirts and bathing-suit tops.

The grounds were decorated with palm trees and tropical flowers, and a fountain spouted up in the center of the pool. Another fountain, spewing champagne, was placed at the bar. While I was looking over the scenery, my eyes caught sight of Maribeth. She was tan and wearing an orchid pinned on the left side of her hair, just above her ear. She was talking to some of the guests.

All evening I planned how I would approach her, but I could not build up the courage. Finally, while I was sitting in the sunroom and reading the palms of some of her sisters, Maribeth walked in and plopped herself on the chair next to me. She stretched out her arm and commanded, in a sarcastic tone, that I read her palm.

I had taken some palm reading courses based on Cheiro's famous book, *Palmistry for All,* but I didn't want to bother with that. I took her hand, looked intently at her palm, and told her that she was going to be married before she was 24 and that the man was going to be someone from outside the United States. At that time, she was 19 years old. She made a snide remark, got up, and walked away with a swish of her grass skirt. Her slim, six-foot frame disappeared into the other room.

That was the last I saw of her until several years later, when fate brought us together again.

//////////

On the way home to Afghanistan in September 1969, I stopped over in London to spend a few days with my sister. She was living on the top floor of a huge, multistory house that belonged to an English Lady. One of Salma's friends at college, a young Iranian woman named Shreen, lived in the room across the hall. She was quite attractive, and since we both spoke Farsi, we hit it off right away. So instead of staying a couple of days, I ended up staying for more than a month.

After dinner one night, while the three of us were waiting on the subway platform in Trafalgar Square Station, we heard a commotion and looked up to see two young British thugs beating up a young black boy. He was overpowered and defenseless. Having earned a black belt in karate, I was certain I could break them up and decided to jump in to help the young man. But I could not move. Both of my feet were stuck to the surface of the platform. Looking down, I saw Salma and Shreen hanging on to my ankles, and try as I did, I could not shake them loose. They begged me not to get involved. By the time I dislodged my feet from their grip, I noticed that the victim had pulled out a comb with a sharp pointed handle and stabbed one of his attackers in the hand. Just then the train arrived and the girls pulled me inside.

Salma was very angry, saying that I was insane to try to get involved in someone else's affairs. I told her that I could not stand by and watch someone abuse anyone or anything, and that I was always on the side of the underdog. While I was talking to my sister, I felt Shreen hug my arm, as if to say that she approved of what I had intended to do on the platform.

Over the short period of time that I spent in London, I felt a relationship develop between me and dark-eyed, beautiful Shreen. But I was on my way to Afghanistan, and she was going to be staying in London. We promised to stay in touch.

The night before my departure, we went to a restaurant near Salma's house. Before we entered, I looked up at the sign of the restaurant, which read, THE TWENTY FIFTH HOUR. I did not know why, but somehow that name stuck in my head.

The next morning, I caught a Pan American flight to Beirut, where I spent two days at the Phoenicia Hotel. Beirut was considered the Paris of the Middle East and its financial center. I then caught an Ariana Afghan Airlines flight to Kabul.

A great number of family and friends had turned up at the airport to greet me. After hugs and kisses, we all returned to my parents' house, where more guests were waiting for us. Even though I was tired after my long flight, custom required that I stay up until the last guest left. It was a small price to pay. I was home.

CHAPTER 3

RETURN OF THE PRODIGAL PRINCE

In 1970, the population of Kabul numbered roughly 600,000. There were about 5,000 cars on the streets, mostly owned by government officials and well-to-do elites. Although there was a wide income gap, even the top earners made far less than those in the west: a government minister would rake in a salary of about 10,000 afghanis a month ($200 US), and a servant was paid between 500 to 1,000 afghanis per month ($10 to 20 US). The exchange rate against the US dollar was approximately 50 to 1.

Afghanistan was ruled by French-educated Mohammed Zahir Shah, who had ascended the throne in 1933 at the tender age of 19 upon the assassination of his father, Mohammed Nadir Shah. During the early part of his rule, the country had made some strides to catch up with Western civilization. Kabul University was established in the second decade of his reign in 1946. Between 1953 to 1963, economic development programs were implemented under the prime ministership of Mohammed Daoud, a first cousin of the king. These programs ranged from land reclamation and hydroelectric schemes to small industries and communications systems. But the country's prosperity still rested in agriculture and exports, mainly dried fruits, *karakul* (lamb's wool), and carpets.

The 1950s and 1960s also marked a period of remarkable advances in infrastructure. Wide paved highways enabled traders to travel distances in hours that used to take days. Air service to provincial cities and international flights from east to west meant the country could accommodate a steady increase of tourists.

Dramatic social changes had also taken place, most notably the voluntary shedding of the veil by Afghan women in 1959. But Kabul remained a lethargic city. Entertainment in the Afghan capital was limited to a few kebab joints, teahouses, stuffy embassy parties, and one movie-theater that screened outdated spaghetti westerns.

///////////

MAY 1970

It was another Thursday evening in Kabul. A Thursday like any other. Friday was the Sabbath day, so it was the start of the weekend in Afghanistan, as it is in most Islamic countries. I asked myself where to go and what to do. Where the heck was the party?

During the day the streets had been overtaken by peddlers, camel caravans, and bedraggled hippies. Now, the streets were empty and desolate. The flat-roofed, mud-brick structures that looked like *nan* (bread) baking in the afternoon sun seemed to vanish in the pale moonlight. One might say the city ceased to exist after 8 p.m.

I was sitting with a couple of my cousins at the Khyber Restaurant in the fashionable Sher-e-Now district. By Western standards, the place was a dingy eatery. In Kabul, it was a respectable establishment. Hoping that something exciting might turn up, I was dressed in a crisp white shirt and khakis. I still sported a goatee and absurdly bushy sideburns. I had a certain air about me that suggested I had just come back from an extended trip abroad. I had taken a peek at the world outside, and now my hometown looked like a bland, lifeless settlement.

My cousins and I were the only patrons in the government-owned restaurant. Shrill Indian music was playing in the background from an old Japanese tape deck. The sound was sorely grating on my nerves. Having spent almost four exciting and adventurous years in the United States, I had forgotten just how uneventful life could be in Kabul. Had I remembered, I might have stayed at the university for a master's degree.

The Khyber Restaurant, and a handful of similar venues, was the extent of Kabul's nighttime entertainment for the Afghan elite and the small expatriate community, mostly diplomats, contractors, and their families. The restaurant was a large hall with a capacity to seat about 500 people, who would fetch their food from a cafeteria-like annex. They served Afghan food—kebabs, rice, and stewed vegetables. The set-up was hardly glamorous, a far cry from the swanky nightspots I had frequented in the States. Construction work on the Intercontinental Hotel had not yet been completed, and even though the Kabul Hotel was operational, it offered nothing that would appeal to the city's privileged youngsters, who had travelled abroad and seen the best of the West.

This is sad, I thought disgustedly, doodling on a corner of the *Kabul Times*, the local English daily. There must be something better to do than hang around here drinking green tea. If I wanted to drink green tea, I would have stayed at home.

Cousin Abdullah Rassoul, who was about my age, and Khalil, who was much older, were quite happy being there. This was their hangout and they had no qualms about it. Rassoul and I had always been close. We attended the same French Academy and were in the same class. Cousin Khalil, the son of my uncle King Enyatullah, was much older and had spent his growing up years in Tehran after his family left Afghanistan during the 1929 revolution. He was glad to be back among the family and did not complain much. He just watched us with a knowing smile on his face.

It was rather depressing to see three bachelors of royal blood, who could have had anything they wanted in the country, sitting sipping tea.

They asked me about my life in the United States and I told them about the discos, the bars, the beautiful women, and drinking real drinks: Black Label scotch, dry vodka martinis. Khalil quietly shook his head in disapproval. He was in his mid-fifties, the eldest son of my uncle, King Inayatullah Khan[1], and more like an uncle to us, but young at heart. He remarked that discotheques in Kabul were

---

1 Amir Inayatullah Khan (b.1888-1946) was king for three days after the abdication of his brother Amir Amanullah Khan. He was deposed on January 17, 1929, by Habibullah Ghazi (a.k.a. "Batchay Sakau").

a pipe dream. He said that Afghan society would never accept such an establishment.

As I looked down on my doodling, I realized that I had drawn the floor plan of the Twenty-Fifth Hour Restaurant where Salma, Shreen, and I had had dinner on the last night of my stay in London.

I looked at my cousins and with determination in my voice told them that I was going to build Kabul's first disco and that I was going to call it the 25 Hour Key Club.

They both looked at me as if I had lost my mind. They told me that if I was so unhappy, maybe I should go back to the States. I told them that instead of my going to the States, I would bring a part of US culture to Afghanistan.

Khalil told me that I would be run out of town, that the family would never approve of such a venture, and Abdullah agreed. I told them that they were underestimating the people of the town. I asked them what they would be doing that evening if they had a choice between going to a disco and sitting at the Khyber restaurant, sipping tea. They both answered in one voice that they would definitely choose the disco.

Banging my fist on the table, I shouted that the decision was made. I was going to build Afghanistan's first discotheque.

My two cousins listlessly rolled their eyes and said that I was on one of my rampages again. That I would get over it. They both ordered another pot of tea.

Of course, that did it. It was clearly a challenge, and my pride was at stake. Was I not a grandson of King Habibullah Khan[2], the great reformer whose Western outlook brought much-needed improvements to the stodgy ways of traditional Afghan society? Habibullah had instituted a French educational system in Kabul, introduced modern scientific innovations, and offered his people a relaxed style of governance. But I was also a Leo. Had they not been my relatives, I might have roared in the face of this test of their audacity.

Getting up and bidding them good night, I assured them that I would have a disco built within two months. I turned on my heels and walked out the door, the soles of my shoes screeching on the pale green linoleum floor. I could not wait to get out of that suffocating place.

---

2 Amir Habibullah Khan (b.1872-d.1919), ruler of Afghanistan from 1901 to 1919. He introduced much-needed reforms and steered his country on a moderate political course.

The wind chimes hanging over the doorframe tinkled for a few moments after I left the restaurant. They mingled with my thoughts as I wondered how my future, and in fact Afghanistan's future, would be changed if I went through with my plan.

////////////

The next morning I woke up very early. I had my customary morning tea and a piece of freshly baked flatbread with cheese. Then I hopped into my older brother Abdullah's white Ford, since I did not have my own set of wheels, and roared into the city. I was a man on a mission. I needed to find suitable premises for my project.

Ever since my return from the States my father had been on my back to find a decent job and make something of myself. He told me that it was my duty to the Seraj family to find a respectable position, perhaps in a government department, or at the very least, to start a respectable business. This was expected of all the boys from noble families. He suggested that with my agricultural background he could call the Minister of Agriculture on my behalf. I thanked him politely and told him that I was not interested in such a position as my heart was not in it. I did not see myself in a government post. My father had been with the Ministry of Commerce for a long time before serving as the commercial attaché at the Afghan Embassy in Pakistan for many years. He was happy with his work, but I knew that a desk job was not for me. It was too sedate. Respectability was not high on my agenda. I was what my European friends would have called a *bon vivant*. I knew I was a disappointment to my parents in many ways. Although I wished for their sake I could conform to their exigencies, I was not one to compromise, especially on my own happiness.

But what if my parents were right? What if there were no alternatives open to me apart from a banal government desk job? What then? Live out the rest of my years in a humdrum, predictable existence?

While these thoughts were going through my mind I noticed that the gas gauge was almost on empty, so I stopped at a gas station. And it was then that I saw the magic words "For Rent" posted up against two adjoining shops across the street. Immediately, I ran over to find the owner of the property.

It so happened that the owner was none other than my cousin, Salah Ghazi, whose mother was half-sister to my father. Salah's grandmother had hailed from Nuristan[3] province in northeast Afghanistan, and he had inherited the distinct features of the Nuristani[4] people. He had an olive complexion, high cheekbones, and a straight nose. From his father's side, he was also a cousin of King Zaher Shah.

This turned out quite well, since I was virtually penniless and hoped that Salah would give me a break and allow a grace period to pay the rent and security deposit. Salah, like me, was an adventurer. He despised conformity and was a lady's man. He was a hunter and always looking for new adventures.

The prospect of a nightclub on his property tickled him, albeit he doubted I would go ahead with it. But my persistence paid off, and within a day the deal was sealed. Salah even agreed to my terms and conditions, and gave me the keys to the two shops to do with as I pleased. But something had to be done and fast, because according to the "terms and conditions," I only had a couple of months to come up with the money.

///////////

I went into business scarcely an hour after my cousin handed over the keys to me. I contacted two carpenter brothers who had been in the service of my family for many years and spent the rest of the day at the premises, conjuring up possible designs for the new venue. It had to be grand, and it had to have shock value. Subtlety was not my style. It had to be brash. It had to be loud. It had to shake the foundations of Kabul society because, quite frankly, Kabul needed to be shaken up. I could see a flashing signboard. I could see disco lights. I could taste the dry vodka martinis. I could hear the beat of the music. I was tapping my foot.

3   Nuristan refers to the area of Laghman and Ningrahar. Until the late 19th century, the region was known as Kafiristan ("Land of Infidels") because the inhabitants were non-Muslim. Between 1985 and 1900, King AbdurRahman sent numerous expeditions into Kafiristan and finally succeeded to convert the inhabitants. He then renamed the region Nuristan ("Land of Light") as they had now seen the light of Islam.
4   Nuristanis are believed to be the descendants of the ancient Greeks, following the expedition of Alexander the Great (327 BCE-325 BCE) into what is now Afghanistan.

The next morning I took the carpenters to the premises, and as they walked through the door I slipped off my shoelaces and tied them together. I asked one of the perplexed brothers to hold one end of the lace against the centre of the wall, which divided the two shops. With the other end of the lace, I drew a large circle on the white wall. After completing the circle, I told the carpenters that as a first step they should break down the wall along the circular line to create an archway. The brothers nodded silently with a question mark on their brows, as they could not fathom what I intended to do with the place.

Next, going to the corner of the room, I drew a curvy line in the dust on the floor and told the brothers to mark it. I planned to have a bar built in the shape of a half pear. The brothers again nodded, this time looking even more confused.

Since both brothers had grown up within our household, I knew that money was not an issue. I also knew that what I was asking was within their expertise and ability.

I then asked them to arrange to purchase the raw material on a credit basis and to start work that very same day. Before I could finish my sentence, one of the brothers was out of the door and on his way to fulfil my instructions. No more words were needed. The brothers wanted no assurances. No guarantees. The word of a prince was as good as gold. The Seraj family had been good to them over the years.

They started work that morning.

By that afternoon, the ruckus of the affair had drawn the attention of passersby. Hammering and drilling were not common sounds in the normally quiet district across the Sher-e-Now Park. Kabul was a small town, and word travelled fast.

Next to these two shops was a perfumery owned and operated by a 30-something Frenchman named Gerard LeFevre. Slim, with dark brown hair, deep blue eyes, and a perpetual smirk on his clean-shaven face, Gerard had an arrogant attitude and was in partnership with an absentee Afghan businessman. A few days later, he paid me a visit in the midst of the construction to make inquiries. The Frenchman leaned against the doorway, dressed in a loose white t-shirt over cotton khakis and smoking his customary Gitane cigarette. He studied the scene for some time. No one noticed his presence until, it would seem, he decided to make them notice.

Before he could ask me anything, I told him that I was building a discotheque. He could not believe his ears, so he asked me if what he heard was correct. Impatiently, I answered yes. I did not have time for chitchat. I told him that I would tell him more at the end of the day. He scowled and left.

Gerard was a well-known fixture in Kabul society, as I found out. He had moved to Afghanistan a few years back when I was still in the States. No one knew exactly what brought him to the country. He simply claimed to "like it here." He spoke fluent Dari (albeit with a distinct French accent) and had even converted to Islam. As such, he had adopted the Muslim name "Abdullah," but most people still preferred to call him by his Christian name, especially the ladies.

In addition to the two carpenters, I also hired a tinsmith and ordered him to manufacture a neon sign in the shape of a key, with the name "25 Hour Club" lit in blue.

There was a lot of activity taking place when Gerard entered the shops. After the standard pleasantries, the Frenchman plunged directly into the matter at hand. He wanted to know under what name I was going to open the disco, and when I told him, he shook his head knowingly and exhaled a stream of smoke. His cool blue eyes never betrayed any enthusiasm. He said nothing but smiled and tilted his head to the side. He appeared to be saying that I was at the start of something bigger than anything that had ever happened in Kabul.

My debts were fast mounting. The rent, security deposit, wages for two carpenters and a tinsmith, cost of decoration and furniture— all to be imported from Europe, Pakistan, and China—and the salary of the staff I had yet to hire all amounted to a small fortune. And there was still no nightclub to generate any revenue.

One night while I was pondering my financial situation, it came to me like a thunderbolt. Since I had named my discotheque a club, I decided to make it into a private club, which would require patrons to buy membership cards. This would not only help raise funds for the development of my club, but would also keep the riff-raff out of the premises. Satisfied with my newfound solution, I went to bed.

The next morning, I went to the government press house and commissioned the design and printing of the cards. The small, folded cards were white on the inside with blue flaps. I decided to charge 500 afghanis per member (about $10), provided an individual purchased the card before the opening of the club. Those who bought memberships after that would be charged 5,000 afghanis ($100). That hefty price increase would encourage people to buy in before we opened, but the early-bird fee itself was far from cheap. For 500 afghanis, an entire family could dine at a reputable restaurant.

I went to visit friends and associates at their workplaces, homes, and even at the Khyber Restaurant. It did not take much effort to sell the membership cards. As word got around, people even came to see me to purchase their cards. Within a week, I had sold about 200 memberships.

Soon I had a visit from a carpet dealer I knew named Tahir. His family manufactured and exported Afghan tapestries to Europe and ran a shop opposite the Ministry of Interior on the street parallel to my club. Tahir, who was in his mid-twenties and had curly black hair and olive skin, had studied in Germany and travelled extensively for trade. He was driving past in his beige Mercedes when he came to a screeching halt. I was standing outside the club supervising the workers as they erected the large neon sign that read "The 25 Hour Club."

After hearing my plans for the club, Tahir was very interested in a partnership in the project, so I sold him 15 percent interest in the club for 200,000 afghanis ($4,000). He left with a promise to bring in the money the next day. The following day, he made good on his word and delivered the cash. He did not ask for, nor did I offer to give him a receipt. My family name was a good enough receipt for any type of transaction. I added his funds to the 100,000 afghanis I had already made on the sale of the membership cards.

When Gerard found out that I had taken on a partner, he offered me 50,000 afghanis ($1,000) to join in. I offered him 5 percent interest plus a management position. I figured that having a European as a manager would draw the foreign community to the club. Now I had considerable liquid assets to invest in my project, and no expense was spared to turn The 25 Hour Club into a Shangri-La.

A few weeks earlier, I had a dream. I watched now as this dream materialized before my very eyes. Under my meticulous, uncompromising guidance, my workmen had transformed the two adjoining shops in the quiet district of Sher-e-Now into a visual feast of velvet walls, cascades of stainless steel, silk upholstery, leather stools, and a bar festooned with gilded rhinestones.

The floors were covered in pale grey wall-to-wall carpeting. The walls near the bar were decorated with stainless steel tiles evoking a gushing waterfall. The front of the bar was swathed in black leather with gold thumbtack designs, and placed before it were matching leather barstools and footrests.

Speakers were placed along the deep maroon velvet-covered walls in the barroom and the main room. The seats were scalloped with red and gold Chinese silk. At the center, a ceramic tile dance-floor was concealed under a deep red Afghan *Mauri*[5] carpet. I placed the carpet figuring that the sight of a dance-floor might give some of the old guard a heart attack.

Even among the more "progressive" families, there were still many who believed in segregating wedding parties because "good girls" should not make spectacles of themselves by dancing before a male audience. While I, like my uncle King Amanullah, believed strongly in women's freedom and equality to men, I decided it would be best to dole out the shock factor in measured doses. After all, it would have done me no good to be shut down by governmental decree—or worse, Islamic *fatwa*—on opening night! I had learned this lesson from our family's history: King Amanullah's program on westernizing Afghanistan was touted as anti-Islamic and led to a revolution, which resulted in my uncle abdicating the throne.

Therefore, even though there was a barroom, I did not intend to serve alcohol for the first couple of weeks. There were many Afghans who would disapprove. Instead, we would just offer juices, sodas, and non-alcoholic cocktails. The consumption of alcohol was a sin, according to Islam, and while many Afghans did enjoy a glass or three, it was best to enjoy it privately.

Past the archway was the dining area, and farther along stood another smaller bar where alcohol would eventually be served. This intimate bar was intentionally built away from the door for discretion. It was decorated in the manner of an old English pub with glasses hanging above the bartender.

---

5   Mauri design refers to the small octagonal "Tekke gul" design on a fine carpet, a medallion shape named after a Turkmen tribe. It is mostly woven in the northwestern Afghan province of Herat.

The kitchen was designed for preparing Afghan food and equipped with wood-burning stoves. The waiters were outfitted in red silk tunics with wide sashes and baggy black pants. The staff hailed from various parts of Afghanistan. I employed young men regardless of their tribal affiliation, whether Pushtoon, Tajik, Uzbek, or Hazara.

I was very pleased with myself. Life was about to take a major turn in Kabul. What I promised my cousin Abdullah and Khali was now about to burst open on the unsuspecting community of Kabul. To hell with all the naysayers!

I was very selective in hiring the employees of the club. The first hired were two brothers named Aziz and Rashid. I made Aziz the headwaiter and Rashid a bartender. Since Rashid was not familiar with alcoholic beverages, I took it upon myself to teach him all I knew. He was a very good student and soon learned the business better than I expected. He could unscrew the cap of a whisky bottle with one twist of his palm. I hired two body builders as club security guards, and when my staffing was complete I had a total of twenty employees.

CHAPTER 4

SOCIAL REVOLUTION

AUGUST 1970

The grand opening of The 25 Hour Club marked the dawning of a new era in Kabul, a natural progression of the king's liberalized policies and the easing up of the state security apparatus. A cosmopolitan society began to flourish as the Afghan elite openly socialized with expatriates.

In those first weeks, however, we saw signs of unrest among segments of the local population. The demonstrations, which had begun on the campus of the university and in Kabul's secondary schools, quickly spread to the provinces where farmers were suffering from a two-year drought. Riots became more and more frequent and the king was openly criticized. Some of the demonstrations went so far as to feature a dog wearing a tag bearing the name "Zaher Shah."

Since the 1950s, young Afghans were sent to Soviet Russia to complete their studies in various fields—but mostly for military training. These young men returned to Afghanistan impressed with the idea of social equality and other "radical" Marxist notions.

Frustrated by America's insistence that Afghanistan resolve its differences with Pakistan, Mohammed Daoud, who was appointed prime minister in 1953, had further steered the country towards the

Soviet sphere. Important infrastructure projects were given to Russian firms, and Russian educators were brought over to Kabul. But Daoud's autocratic mode of governance eclipsed his agenda to develop the economy and force Afghanistan into the 20th century. In March 1963, the prime minister was forced to resign.

In 1964, the king had ratified a new constitution that allowed, for the first time in Afghanistan's history, the formation of political parties—provided those parties' aims conformed to the fundamental principles of the constitution: Islam, monarchy, and individual freedom. This clause effectively barred Marxist groupings from forming legitimate political parties. Moreover, the new constitution specifically forbade members of the royal family from holding cabinet posts in order to prevent Daoud Khan from regaining office.

Daoud retreated into the shadows with his following of "Young Turks" and began dealings with left-wing dissidents. Thus, it was in the midst of the king's liberalization policies that the foundations of a communist party were quietly laid.

////////////

Such political issues were not on our minds on The 25 Hour Club's opening night. We were focused on making our own history. The grand opening of Afghanistan's first discotheque was a historic event, not only in Kabul, but also on an international scale.

The first guest to arrive was my cousin and best friend and the person who made it possible for me to undertake such an enormous risk, Salah Ghazi. He walked in, attired in a stylish Italian suit and cravat, and exclaimed how amazed he was at what I had accomplished in such a short time. He looked over the chic surroundings and wished me luck. We both knew that I needed all the luck in the world to make the club a success. I was entering uncharted waters, building a bridge to a new era. There was no turning back.

Outside, there was a great deal of commotion as cars drove up from all directions. Amid the tranquility of the night was the sound of purring engines, feet shuffling on the pavement, and the hum of polite conversation. On the sidewalk, a large sign on a tripod stated that it was a private party and only those with invitations could come in.

A dozen young men dressed in dark suits were guarding the entire area. They kept vigil for undesirables who may attempt to enter without invitations and cause trouble. As such, there were many who were turned away at the door. Word had gotten around. Too many curiosity-seekers wanted to see what all the commotion was about.

Those who were granted access found themselves stepping into a room incandescent with candles. It was opulence like they had never known it. The solid brass lampshades lent a golden hue to the premises and the maroon velvet walls evoked a delicate richness. The tables set up along the wall were replete with savory dishes. The amount of food on display might have seemed obscene to those unaccustomed to Afghan hospitality. Food—an overabundance of food—is a staple for greeting guests. There should always be more food than the party can possibly consume. An empty plate is a disgrace, a dishonor. A poor farmer would slaughter his last sheep to feed an unexpected visitor. As for a prince, anything less than a munificent feast would be viewed as a deliberate affront. So, I went all out to set up a most elaborate menu, straight out of my grandfather's personal palace cookbook.

The scent of French perfume favored by most aristocratic Afghan women mingled with the tantalizing aroma of Afghan gastronomical delights: rice dishes, stews, stuffed vegetables, and a variety of skewered meats. The waiters, bearing silver trays full of finger foods, slivered through the crowd, dodging cigarettes and glasses filled with Coca Cola or orange juice.

The hall was abuzz with conversation. The men were dressed in finely tailored suits, the ladies clad in figure-hugging evening gowns and adorned with dazzling gems. Members of all the noble families were present, including the Tarzis, Charkhis, and Etemadis, to name a few. There was Prince Nader, the king's second eldest son; cabinet ministers; the mayor of Kabul; foreign diplomats; prominent businessmen; and a slew of my kin, including my younger sister Salma and her husband, Tamim Etemadi, son of Prime Minister Nourahmad Etemadi.

Overnight, the club became a national and international success.

One month after the opening I started serving wine and soon thereafter offered a full bar. The religious leaders did not raise any objections, as the club "served" alcoholic beverages to the foreign community only.

From 1970 to the spring of 1973, the club became the center of an international who's who list. It catered to prominent visitors like the Crown Prince of Japan and his wife when they were on an official visit to Afghanistan. Regular guests included members of the diplomatic communities, writers such as Leon Uris and Joseph Kassel, movie actors, U.S. Marine guards from the American Embassy, United Nations personnel, and members of various intelligence agencies like the MI6, KGB, CIA, and Iranian Todeh. Since our venue was the hub, all these agencies wanted to know what the others were doing.

The club paved the way to a new and free society. The fashions among the ladies followed their European counterparts, including miniskirts, hot pants, and the latest makeup styles. Kabul became a favourite stopover point for the hippies of the world on their way to Kathmandu.

Among the many visitors and guests was a mysterious German man by the name of Heinz. He offered to design and build a glass dance floor with multicolored lights underneath at the club. He offered to do this for free as long as he could eat his meals at the club without charge.

His offer was too good to be ignored, so I accepted, and within one week of working nights he did as he promised. The club now featured a glass dance floor with 250 lights blinking to the sound of the music, predating the famed lit dance floor that would come to New York City's Club 54. Years later, I found out that Heinz worked for the East German secret police, and ever since then I have often wondered how many listening devices he had installed around the club.

To complement the new dance floor, I hired a rock band made up of a Spanish organist, two Pakistani guitarists, an Afghan drummer, and a vocalist from India.

Until its completion, I continued to cover the dance floor with an Afghan carpet. The night of inauguration, when the band started to play, I sent two waiters over to roll up the rug. As soon as the rug was removed, I turned on the dance floor lights and the band broke into a tune by Santana. All hell broke loose. People jumped out of their seats and the dance floor became jammed with gyrating bodies. To make things more exciting, I turned on the black light that was strategically attached over the dance floor. The Afghan crowd had never seen anything like it, and the ladies wearing white bras beneath their black tops became exposed. Some ran off the dance floor, hugging their chests, while others continued dancing without a care. The Social Revolution was born that night and I became the king of nightlife in Afghanistan. Kabul had come alive.

CHAPTER 5

SPIES IN OUR MIDST

FALL 1972

Among the regulars at the club were three Soviet Russians—Constantine, Alex, and Victor. This trio seemed to have no purpose in Kabul apart from spending a few nights a week at The 25 Hour Club, drinking countless glasses of Stolichnaya.

On occasion, the three would walk in holding bottles of vodka and insist that I drink a few "grams" of vodka with them. A few grams to them added up to almost a full glass. They would start toasting to my health, the king's health, and anyone else they could think of. By the time they got to the doorman at the club, I was totally under the table, so to speak. I was amused at their behavior. I knew full well that they worked for the KGB.

Kabul had become spy central. Afghanistan was located at the crossroads of politically ambitious nations, covertly maneuvering to further their own agendas from within the country. Close to the oil-rich Persian Gulf and the Indian Ocean ports, it bordered Iran in the west and Pakistan in the south and east. In the north, it shared a border with the Muslims of the Soviet Union's Central Asian republics. After holding a neutral position in the Second World War, King Zaher

Shah sought to realize a policy of nonalignment, independence, and development. But in the background, darker forces were at play.

For Moscow, a friendly Afghanistan was vital; for Washington, it was imperative that Moscow be kept in check. During the détente period of the Cold War, clandestine agents—or spies—mainly operated out of official installations such as embassies or military bases. But there were also people in the markets, countryside, and other "social" environments. Aerial imaging and electronic intercepts could only reveal so much. Human sources could reveal thought patterns and intentions.

The KGB played an important role in furthering Soviet foreign policy objectives abroad. In addition to straightforward intelligence collection and counterintelligence, the KGB participated in the Kremlin's program of active measures. The bureau recruited, trained, and assigned KGB officers to foreign countries under false identities or diplomatic cover. Soviet civilians stationed abroad, whether as correspondents, trade representatives, or Aeroflot clerks, were strictly watched.

The Chinese were in Afghanistan to monitor Soviet advances in the region. Since the 1960s, Beijing competed with Moscow for political influence among communist parties and in the developing world in general. Following the Soviet invasion of Czechoslovakia in 1968 and clashes on the Sino-Soviet border in 1969, Chinese competition with the Soviet Union increasingly reflected concern over China's own strategic position.

Since the 1970s, East Germany pursued an active policy in the Third World to advance its own specific interests and as part of its role as a Soviet client. The "Stasi" or SSD (Staatssicherheitsdienst "State Security Service") was East Germany's equivalent of the KGB.

At the crossroads of so many interests, Afghanistan was an ideal location to gather information. I had been warned about the Russian trio by a Lebanese businessman called Willy, who referred to them as "the three stooges." Willy was a regular at the club and enjoyed sharing his insights about the cloak-and-dagger world we lived in. He told me that any Russian who was working or visiting abroad had to be KGB, otherwise he would never have been granted permission to leave the Soviet Union. No Russian would dare to move so freely and behave so rashly, unless he was instructed to do so. It was true that the three Russians were a lively bunch, even if they were communists. They were young, inseparable, and even looked alike, and to the casual observer they appeared harmless. After a few drinks, however, they came alive, and their bland faces took on a measure of individuality. Alex was the boss, Victor was his second-in-command, and Constantine was the lackey.

Willy ran an exporting company in Kabul. He had lived in Iran for two years before coming to Kabul earlier in the year, and had managed to make friends with the who's who within a short period of time. He owned the only shipping and forwarding company in Kabul and thus was very much sought after by the foreign community who either were entering or leaving Afghanistan.

I believed it was important to maintain a pleasant ambiance at the club, even if some of my patrons were unsavory characters. My policy was to keep my antennas up and keep myself out of trouble. I assigned a young college graduate by the name of Farhad to keep his ears and eyes open for any suspicious activity. I also contacted a friend who was a top diplomat at the American Embassy and apprised him of my concerns.

One evening, the trio boss, Alex, extended me an invitation to see a Russian ballet performance. After watching the show at the National Theatre, the three Russians invited me backstage to meet the prima ballerina, who had the face of an angel and soft, lustrous, jet-black hair. She was stunningly beautiful. Her priceless assets were set off to perfection by a shimmering gown with a plunging décolletage and skin-tight bodice, bedecked with pearls and sequins. Katyusha was peeled out of any man's fantasy.

The trio were attempting to convince me that she liked me. This ice maiden with a commanding presence and steel-grey eyes that could pierce through a man's soul was sipping on a glass of mango juice that Constantine had brought her. Victor kept a lookout for any eavesdroppers. Alex drew nearer, and whispered in my ear that she liked me very much.

While I was listening to Alex's whispers, I heard the sound of glass breaking. Looking around, I saw that Katyusha had dropped her glass and her pearly dress was splattered with bright orange stains. Alex told her to go and change her dress. Without responding to Alex, she turned her eyes and fixed her icy gaze on me and asked me to help her change, since her makeup artist had gone home. As she spoke, she extended a creamy white arm towards me. Alex insisted that I should help her.

Help her? I snapped out of my fantasy mode. What did she want from me? The three stooges seemed overly eager—suspiciously overeager. It took every nerve and muscle in my body to respectfully decline the woman's offer. Russia's beauties were a deadlier asset of the Soviet Union than its nuclear arsenal.

Many a powerful man, including a number of Afghan cabinet ministers, were spellbound by a KGB agent in lipstick and stilettos. I was a prince and in a position to know the "ins and outs" of Afghanistan's affairs. Being a member of the royal family and having relatives who held high-ranking posts in the military, the right woman could glean a great deal of information if she could take me as a lover. I would be a madman and a traitor to my country if I engaged in a tryst with such a woman.

I excused myself and said that I had spent enough time with them. Bidding them good night, I hastily made my exit to avoid enduring one more minute of temptation.

/////////

It would not be the first or last time a Russian beauty would attempt to use her feminine guiles in wooing me to the other side of the Iron Curtain. Albeit, some offers were easier to refuse than others, but refuse I did.

One night, while I was standing near the bar of the club talking to Willy, he whispered that Fred and Ginger had just walked in. He had given this name to the Russian couple who was entering the club because they could dance like Fred Astaire and Ginger Rogers. In addition to the "three stooges" and the Aeroflot staff, Willy now brought to my attention this peculiar twosome who frequented the club "under the guise" of man and wife. At least, Willy was convinced it was a guise.

Whenever a patron from the Allied world entered the scene, whether American, British, French, or West German, "Fred and Ginger" would appear. The couple would dance together once, and then split up. The man would mingle with the ladies and his "wife" would invite some of the prominent Afghan men to dance with her.

Willy enjoyed his Scotch whisky. He knew more about the foreign community in Kabul than anyone else. I used to tease him by saying that I could save a lot of money if I could collect his showering water and distill it, because it would be pure alcohol.

Along with the rest of the affluent foreigners in the country, Willy's origins were shrouded in mystery. In Kabul, it was best not to hold anyone's personal life against him. Ultimately, everyone thought the other was a spy—or some other important figure that transcended his "undercover persona." The Afghans thought the foreigners were undercover agents; the foreigners thought the Afghan elite were national intelligence. Everyone suspected the lower-class Afghans were informants. As for the lower-class Afghans, no one cared what they thought.

The 25 Hour Club was located a half-block away from the Aeroflot (Russian National Airline) office on Chicken Street. The airline staffers were an airtight bunch, but they were regulars at the club. The girls never went out without the managers, who served as their male chaperones. Or, on certain occasions, they were all seen with officials from the Russian embassy. They popped in to the club every so often, simply to see who was there, who was with whom, and what was going on. It was their only opportunity to scout the area outside of working hours, beyond the confines of their office and with a justifiable excuse.

Moments after the Aeroflot staff entered the club, a couple of Americans invariably walked in. This was the routine. If the Russians sat at the bar, the Americans settled at a table nearby, within earshot. Soon after the Americans walked in, another set of European men would walk in. Among them was a man from Britain, whom I shall call Jerry, and his wife Nancy. Again, my unappointed agent Willy told me that the Brits were members of MI6.

My cousin Salah and I referred to the Americans, Europeans, and British at these tables as "the cavalry." Salah did not trust Gerard, even though the Frenchman's behaviour at the club was usually beyond reproach. He kept to his own except when he went table to table to make sure everyone was satisfied with the service. And then he retreated to his dark corner by the bar to smoke a Gitane and observe the cotillion. He did not engage in excessive conversation with one party, but instead divided his attention equally among all the patrons, no matter their nationality.

I dismissed my cousin's assessment. Gerard was nothing but an unnerving Frenchman, and there was nothing I could do about it. To charge Gerard of taking part in insidious activities without any concrete evidence would only humiliate his accuser. One evening, however, I saw Gerard engrossed in a conversation with Heinz, who stopped by the club fairly often to claim his free meals. In the course of these visits, Heinz would offer to look over the wiring in the "sound and light" room. He explained that it was necessary to inspect "*zee system*" from time to time to prevent a malfunction or short circuit. Gerard usually attended to these matters as I avoided dealing with technicalities.

The Frenchman did have a few redeeming qualities. For instance, he was exceedingly popular with the ladies, and there were many who tried to chat him up. Gerard had the aura of a European film star, elegant and elusive. He had a handsome face with refined features, and his easy sophistication, devoid of flashy clothing or expensive accessories gave him an air reminiscent of the French actor Alain Delon. He spoke very little about himself and was extremely attentive to others. These qualities were especially fascinating to the ladies who frequented the club.

One evening while I was leaning against the archway, enmeshed in my own thoughts, "Ginger" extended her invitation to dance with me. "Fred" was nowhere in sight. I looked at the tall, voluptuous blond. She was in excellent form. Her arms were muscular and she had a stunning figure. The expression on her face seemed to suggest she did not expect a rejection. No one ever rejected her invitation to "*dunce.*"

But I did, as politely as I could.

She insisted. My eyes slowly scanned the woman, from her painted toes to the roots of her hair. The roots needed retouching. She was no blond, and certainly not a seductress. She was a sham. Ginger needed to work on her act. Again, I refused and walked away. She mumbled something in Russian, which I am sure was not complimentary.

///////////

Hearsay carried a lot of weight at the height of the Cold War, especially in eastern lands where word-of-mouth was a tried, tested, and true method of long-distance communication. Much as in cities across North America, in Kabul the gossip fueled the hysteria over the presence of spies in its midst.

One evening while I was closing the club's accounts for the evening, Sarwar, my burly bodyguard, came into the office and grumbled under his breath that he had been hearing things that needed my immediate consideration. He did not often have something to say, but when he did, he insisted upon the *sardar's* (my) undivided attention.

Sarwar closed the office door behind him, looked around to make sure no one else was in the room, and quoted an Afghan proverb: "The walls have mice, and the mice have ears."

I was getting impatient and told him that I needed to be somewhere soon. He huffed and then in a very quiet voice told me that he had overheard people saying that they should be careful about what they say in here because the owner has installed listening devices everywhere.

I was dumbfounded by his statement. I did not expect to hear about espionage tactics from my bodyguard, but Sarwar's grasp of Kabul's undercurrents had far exceeded my expectations.

Even though he saw and felt my displeasure at his words, he insisted that he was telling the truth about what he had heard. I told him that the only electronic thing installed since the opening of the club was the electrical lights under the dance floor that Heinz had done.

Without taking his eyes off me he asked me to repeat the name of the installer.

"Heinz, the German guy—" and then, suddenly illuminated, I repeated: "Heinz, the German guy!"

I saw before me Heinz's pale, nondescript face and round, coke-bottle glasses. No one ever quite knew what he was doing in Kabul except attending to odd fix-it jobs. When he came to claim his free meals at the club, he hardly ever spoke to me or anyone else. He restricted his dealings to Gerard.

Immediately, I called out for the Frenchman and relayed Sarwar's information. My bodyguard did not feel it was a wise move to consult the foreigner, but he knew that the *sardar* always acted on impulse. Gerard rejected Sarwar's accusation and compared it to the propaganda campaign waged by British agents in the late 1920s to poison the minds of Afghan peasants against the monarchy. The campaign was successful inasmuch as it brought about the downfall of King Amanullah.

I was hardly convinced by Gerard's argument. I ordered the staff to conduct a thorough search of the premises for any suspicious devices. The search yielded a calculator and a fancy silver lighter, but no devices of any kind were uncovered.

The following morning, I went to call on Willy. The Syrian was knee-deep in all this espionage business. He was in with the American embassy crowd, and always the first to issue "unofficial" warnings about what not to do and whom to avoid.

I asked Willy point blank what he knew about Heinz. I told him that I had heard things that I did not like. He looked at me seriously and asked if I was talking about the club being rigged with listening devices.

Surprised that Sarwar had been right about all the talk, I asked Willy if he knew who was spreading all these lies. He sat down, took a sip from his ever-present glass of Scotch, and said that among the intelligence it was common knowledge. "You might as well turn the club into a recording studio," he said.

He further revealed that the German guy, Heinz, was bad news. Willy told me that Heinz had recently gone to his office to fix something. When Willy asked him which part of Germany he came from, Heinz had said that he came from Gelsenkirchen. Willy said that he had lived most of his life in Germany. He knew it well, and he recognized the regional twangs. "That man did not come from the West," Willy said. "He came from the East."

I asked Willy if he thought Heinz was an East German spy. Willy did not respond to my question except to say that Heinz had left town the day before and probably had dismantled whatever he had installed at the club on his almost nightly inspection of the electrical system that he had installed. I then understood why my people had not found any devices during their search.

Before I left Willy, he shook my hand and said that I should also keep a close eye on Gerard.

//////////

I had always had my doubts about the Frenchman who managed my nightclub. There was no concrete reason for my mistrust. Gerard had never done anything wrong. In fact, he had done nothing but manage the club efficiently, leaving the accounts squeaky clean.

But I prided myself on my instincts, and if my own instincts failed, I began to trust Sarwar's. Sarwar despised Gerard, not that he had done him wrong; on the contrary, Gerard was very fond of my giant. But Sarwar always felt uncomfortable when he was around him. Not only did the six-foot strongman keep a vigilant eye on Gerard's every move, but unbeknownst to me he had also ordered Aziz and Rashid to monitor the Frenchman's goings and comings. If Gerard so much as sneezed during the day, Sarwar would have been able to report at what time and where.

Willy had warned me to keep an eye on the Frenchman's activities in Kabul, and he had confirmed Sarwar's suspicions that Heinz, an unknown German, had rigged the club with listening devices. As a result, apparently, it was widely believed the club was being used by foreign agents to gather intelligence. The contention might not have been true, but everyone *believed* it to be true, and in Kabul, that was better than true.

It was also true that while a slew of similar venues had opened between 1971 and 1972, such as the Blue Club, Shar-e-Gholghola[6], Four Seasons, and Club Number 9, none could provide any real competition. The 25 Hour Club remained the favorite destination for the who's who among the local elite and expatriates, notably diplomats, CEOs, and visiting dignitaries.

Still, I would not believe Gerard was anything more than what he appeared to be: just a pesky Frenchman who was so desperate to gain acceptance by the Afghan aristocracy that he would even change his religion.

My gravest fear was that family members and Afghan officials might now suspect me of being in cahoots with foreign agents, since I

---

6   The Shar-e-Gholghola was named after a city in Bamiyan province, which Genghis Khan burned to the ground because his grandson was slain there. It means "city of screams." The club featured an innovative design, evoking the inside of a cave, and was owned by Shah Wali, who was a famous Afghan singer in the 1960s.

owned The 25 Hour Club. It would be presumed that the owner of the premises had something to do with the bugging. And my extravagant lifestyle must have raised a few eyebrows. I had spared no effort in drawing attention to myself. Only now I realized it might not have been such a good thing, and I contemplated the wisdom of my elders who had always kept a low profile in order not to provoke the masses.

People were probably wondering where I got all my cash. They probably doubted the club could generate so much revenue. When a man was being incriminated, anything under the sun could be misconstrued to make him appear guilty of a crime.

My cousin Salah howled with laughter after listening to my logical deductions. He said that he would pity the spymasters who would enlist me as an agent. "The enemies would hear you driving up a mile away in your Jag!" he said.

I was getting annoyed at Salah's amusement at my expense and demanded to know how a German spy could install bugs in my club right under my nose.

Salah became sober and told me that the answer to my question was that there was a shifty French guy making sure I did not know. I asked Salah if he thought that Gerard was a spy. I told him that Gerard would be nothing without me. He would still be peddling perfume in the corner shop. Salah said that without me he would have found another Afghan to use as a stepping stool. He was convinced that Gerard was up to no good.

My cousin was right. I was neither a spy, nor did I know anything about espionage. But someone at The 25 Hour Club must have known something about espionage. I pondered whether, when it came to Gerard, my bodyguard's instincts may once again have been right.

Gerard was certainly not your average foreigner. He was well spoken, well educated, and well read, with an astonishing knowledge of history and a remarkable understanding of geopolitics. He was also in formidable shape and excelled in various sports. He claimed to love Afghan culture and said he would like to marry an Afghan girl one day. He pledged to live and die in Afghanistan. Naturally, such talk endeared him to the fiercely patriotic Afghan elite.

Did Gerard have a hidden agenda? Sarwar had once said of him, using another Afghan proverb, "Under his bowl, there is a little bowl."

I decided that the best solution to my quandary was not to push the Frenchman away, but to pull him closer. It was not possible to fire him without justifiable grounds. Such things were not done in Kabul, especially to friends of the family, and Gerard, in spite of my misgivings, was considered a friend of the family.

Keep your friends close and your enemies even closer, I reasoned. I invited Gerard to move into one of the many rooms in my multistory building.

CHAPTER 6

A NEW "SILK ROUTE"

The U.S. Embassy in Kabul battled the narcotic trade throughout the Cold War years by helping track down major and minor figures involved in opium trafficking. Although I knew officials from the Embassy and many of the marines who guarded the Embassy were regulars at The 25 Hour Club, my knowledge of the dark underworld of drug running was limited. Until the situation hit close to home.

During the 1970s, Afghan-Pakistani trucking merchants became a growing economic force. A smuggling economy developed, encouraged by the Afghan Transit Trade Agreement made with Pakistan, which enabled landlocked Afghanistan to import selected commodities duty free. Goods were then smuggled back across the border and sold in Pakistan's markets. Pushtoon tribes who straddle the Pakistan-Afghan border controlled the trade. Road construction in the 1970s and investment in heavy trucks with the help of West German credit further facilitated this development.

Another significant dimension of the illicit economy was opium poppy cultivation, which increased in the mid-1970s as opium crops in the so-called Golden Triangle countries declined. Opium poppy has always grown in Helmand and elsewhere in Afghanistan. The crop is easy to cultivate and transport, and offers a quick source of income for impoverished Afghans. In 1972, it was reported that Afghan farmers made $300 to $360 per hectare from opium—twice the average of $175 for fruit.

Throughout history in the Southeast Asian region, the sale of opium had been covertly used by guerrilla fighters and their foreign sponsors to finance resistance efforts against "undesirable" regimes, starting with the Nationalist Chinese Kuomintang's war against Mao's communists in the 1940s and 50s.

But the communist victory in China eliminated the world's major opium market within a decade, and the Asian opium zone contracted geographically. Cold War geopolitics, combined with illicit market forces, stimulated a steady increase in the remaining area, which now stretched from Turkey to Thailand. Supplied by the Asian zone, other markets—particularly in the United States and Iran— expanded their consumption of opiates steadily during this period.

////////////

WINTER 1972

In its second year, The 25 Hour Club was flying on autopilot. The day-to-day operations were left entirely up to the staff, and I made cameos for a couple hours some nights, accompanied by two or three lovely women, and showed up again later to close up. I divided the rest of my attention among a few side businesses I had started, including a bowling alley, taxi company, and tourism agency.

Caravan Travels was born when I realized I was already doing the job for free. Dozens of pretty young things had been given guided tours of the country by a bona fide Afghan prince—at no charge. Perhaps it was my mother's voice ringing in my ears, but I felt it was high time I started charging for my services. Afghanistan was a favorite hippie destination, and an agency specializing in tours of remote provinces and historical sites was much needed.

An office was promptly set up at the back of the club, with ample parking space for rental cars. But the prospect of sitting behind a counter day-in and day-out, fielding calls, and attending to customers did not appeal to me. Gerard graciously offered to do the job since many of the tourists were French and he could better cater to their needs. I was relieved. By this time, Gerard had accepted my offer to move into my building, and he was under Sarwar's unwavering scrutiny, as well as the constant surveillance of Jan-Ali and the staff at the club. If the Frenchman dared to err, my security team would sound the alarm. But there had been no cause for concern—yet.

And then one morning Sarwar knocked on my bedroom door. I was slightly annoyed, as I had closed the club as usual a few hours earlier and was still sleeping. I told Sarwar that whatever he had to say better be good for waking me up so early. Of all my employees, Sarwar was the only one allowed to enter my bedroom, even if I was in bed.

He bowed his head and said that while out to do *oozoo* (washing prior to prayers) at 4 a.m. he saw the *farangi*[7] (Gerard) packing duffle bags into the back of rental cars and sending them off with his girlfriends.

"What girlfriends?" I said. Gerard had no girlfriends to my knowledge. Sarwar repeated that Gerard's girlfriends had piled in the car and a new driver, who was not a member of Caravan Travels, drove the car.

I was stunned. I was too busy to notice that Gerard had not come home last night. Tourists, especially female tourists, never left Kabul in the wee hours of the night, and there were hirelings to help load the bags into the cars. Gerard's behavior was indeed suspicious.

Those days there was a great deal of unexplained phenomena taking place in Kabul. People mysteriously disappeared. Later, it was believed the missing persons had either fled the country or had been arrested by secret agents for whatever questionable business they were charged with dealing in.

Kabulis were high on alert for suspicious activity and anything remotely unusual was perceived as a sign of danger ahead.

I recalled that Aziz had reported some time ago that Gerard would receive visits from French girls at the club during the day, generally customers of Caravan Travels. He would sit with them for some time, and then they would leave. Aziz had insisted these were not friendly visits. He sensed their tone was much too serious.

I had roared with laughter and dismissed my waiter's report. I still did not believe that Gerard could be a spy or up to no good.

---

7   Derogatory term for foreigner, in Pashto.

But now, in light of Sarwar's information, I wondered whether something more sinister was afoot. What was in those duffle bags, and why was Gerard smuggling them out of the country in such a clandestine manner?

I was getting angry by the minute and Sarwar, sensing a violent reaction soon to come from me, suggested that I should not confront the Frenchman immediately, but instead wait until he gave himself away.

"Speak good words to an enemy very softly; gradually destroy him root and branch," he told me, reciting an ancient Pashto proverb. Sarwar was full of proverbs.

/////////////

Judgment day arrived shortly before New Year's Eve. One afternoon, a lone American marine entered the club and walked right up to the bar. Without making any unnecessary small talk, he asked Rashid to tally up the weekly tab.

It was Joe, a marine guard from the Embassy. I just then realized that I had not seen any of the guards for over a week. I found that very strange because they came to the club almost every night, and being good customers they were given the privilege to run a monthly tab.

When I asked him where everyone had been, there was an awkward silence. Without looking at me he stuttered that something had happened and he could not say what—except that they were not allowed to come to the club anymore. He had just come in to settle their tab.

The marine apologized and darted out the door.

My bemusement turned to fury. The marines were regulars at The 25 Hour Club. They came in legions and fired up the place. They drank like fish and ran up an astronomical tab every week. If the U.S. marines were boycotting this club, there had to be a serious reason, and it would not be long before many of his high-profile, big-money patrons would also come up with excuses. Was it because the club catered to the Russians? No, it could not be the Russians; otherwise the Americans would have boycotted the place long ago. And who were they to dictate who should and should not patronize the club, anyway? This was a free country. Something was not right. It had to be a mistake, a misunderstanding.

I hopped into my Jaguar and zoomed over to the U.S. Embassy in the Wazir Akbar Khan district. I knew one of the high officials there, a man I will call Larry Smith. Surely, he would clear things up.

Larry saw me right away, and I told him that I was aware of the club being put off limits to the marines. I said that I had come to personally correct any mistake that may have occurred. Larry apologized and said that it was not a mistake.

He told me that Gerard was the cause of the club being off limits. He informed me that they had Gerard under surveillance and he finally tripped. Holding my temper down, I cursed that son of a bitch under my breath and demanded to know what he had done.

Larry apologized again and said that he was sure that I was not responsible for what Gerard had done, but that they had to "take precautions."

It turned out that Gerard had approached one of the marines and attempted to organize a meeting with Russian officials. The marine had reported the incident to his superiors, and his superiors had taken the matter to the ambassador. The decision was final, and the marines were forbidden from entering The 25 Hour Club.

Larry would not divulge the rest of the data the embassy had compiled on Gerard LeFevre, except to say that the dossier was very thick.

I insisted on knowing whom Gerard was working for. Larry was silent for some time. He took a sip of coffee. And then he looked straight into my eyes and asked me if Gerard ever discussed his ex-wife with me.

I told him that I knew that he was married once, but that was about it. He asked me if I knew who she was. I was getting agitated about this interrogation, and in as calm a voice as I could muster I asked Larry to tell me all he knew. The Embassy's decision to prohibit the marines from attending the club was not going to stay under the rug for long. Kabul was a gossip-mongering city and sooner or later word was going to spread, and that would not bode well for my reputation nor that of my royal family.

Hearing the seriousness in my voice, Larry told me that Gerard was once married to the daughter of a powerful Chinese leader. He dabbled in some very important business. The Embassy knew he was involved in buying and selling information as an independent agent, but until last week they did not think he would attempt to take active measures with an American marine.

I was taken aback. Willy and Salah's suspicions were correct. Gerard had played a part in rigging the club with listening devices. But why had he been loading the rental cars with duffle bags in the middle of the night?

As if reading my mind, Larry informed me that they had reason to believe Gerard was involved in smuggling narcotics.

"That explains the duffle bags in the early morning," I murmured under my breath. Larry looked up at me questioningly and I told him what my staff had reported about Gerard's early morning activities with the duffle bags, cars, and French women.

I decided there and then that I was going to fire the bastard.

Taking another sip of coffee, Larry agreed that that would be a good move. Then he squinted at me as if deep in thought. When he finally spoke up, he said that he had a proposition to make to me. He would have the ambassador lift the boycott of the club if I agreed to help them out.

"What do you want me to do?" I asked.

"We want your people to keep an eye out for drug dealers."

I knew that narcotics posed a huge problem for them and that they were trying to keep tabs on certain people. I smiled and said that I was one step ahead of them. I told him about appointing Farhad to keep an eye on the undesirables. He was a good person and I could also give him the responsibility to do as Larry requested under the condition that the arrangement would be a secret.

"This needs to be just between you and me," I said. "No one else, not even the ambassador, can know anything about it."

Larry got up from behind his desk, came around and hugged me in the Afghan style and promised that no one else would know about what had taken place between us that day.

※※※※※※

Leaving the Embassy, I drove like a madman towards my building. Sarward greeted me when I arrived at the gate. Seeing murder in my eyes, he quickly put his huge hulk in the doorway and begged me to stop for a moment and take some deep breaths. He knew that if I went to Gerard with the rage that was boiling in me I would kill him.

Heeding his advice, I leaned against my car and waited several minutes before going inside, Sarwar close at my heels. Gerard was in his bedroom reading when I kicked his door down. He had a bewildered look on his face as I barged in. I grabbed him by the collar of his shirt, yanked him off the bed, and threw him to the floor, calling him every name in the book. I picked up a chair to crack his head, but Sarwar stepped in between us and held up his hands to take the brunt of the chair coming down.

Waving my fists in the air, I shouted unintelligible phrases, which Sarwar later reminded me were "Russian," "spy," "ex-wife," "Mao Tse-tung," and "drugs."

After I calmed down a bit I felt grateful to Sarwar for stopping me from committing a murder. I stared at the confusion and fear on Gerard's face. He denied having anything to do with drugs. When I asked him about the duffle bags, he told me that they were passengers' bags stuffed with Afghan knick-knacks. Since they wanted an early start, they decided to leave at four a.m. I knew he was lying, but I could not tell him where my information came from. Larry and I had an agreement.

I yelled at him to stop bullshitting me. I said that I knew what he was up to and I wanted him out of building, my club, and my life that very moment. I ordered him to pack his bags and get the hell out of my building.

Gerard was good with words, but he realized nothing he could say would get him out of this mess. He remained quiet for some time, his cheek twitching. His blue eyes studied his opponent, who was heaving loudly.

He made one last attempt to change my mind by telling me how much he believed in me and how he could have helped me become a great leader in Afghanistan.

I turned around and as I walked out I told Sarwar to stay there and make sure that Gerard was out of the building just as soon as he could pack. I went up to my residence and waited for Sarwar to assure me that Gerard was gone.

Within the next few days I made sure that Gerard received my repayment for what he had invested in the club. A few weeks later I learned that he had entered into business with another Afghan.

Gerard continued his illegal activities with some other Afghans. Eventually he was deported from Afghanistan and I was told that he had moved to the Mauritius Islands, where he allegedly died of a heart attack. But rumor has it that he was killed by unknown entities. One could guess who the entity may have been.

CHAPTER 7

BRIDGE TO DESTINY

The Twenty-Five Hour Club was named in *Fodor's Travel Guide to Central Asia* as the most popular place to visit when in Afghanistan, in addition to the InterContinental Hotel.

As the number of people interested in discotheque life increased, more entrepreneurs established new clubs. The newly opened InterContinental Hotel also featured a popular dining facility called The Pamir Restaurant. But none could compete with my club.

In September of 1972, my cousin, Princess Safia Tarzi, who lived in Paris and had a dressmaking business in Afghanistan, came to Kabul for a visit. After seeing my operations, she suggested that I should set up an Afghanistan center in Paris. She told me that one of her close friends was Baron Philippe de Rothschild, a relative of the Rothschild family in the United States. Philippe owned a building across from the George V Hotel off the Champs Élysée, and Safia said she could get the necessary space from him for the Afghan center, provided that she became my partner.

The proposal sounded good and I told her I would seriously think about it. Since the club had taken on a life of its own, I figured going international would not be a bad thing, especially since the French newspaper *Le Figaro* had written a very positive article about The 25 Hour Club and its *patron*, referred to as "its Veritable Prince." A

French TV crew had also done a documentary clip on my club. That kind of publicity would definitely help in the establishment of the Afghan center in Paris.

As October rolled around I was still mulling over Safia's proposal. One evening, while I was entertaining some guests, Safia's sister, Princess Jamila, walked in with a young lady she introduced as Alice McCarey. She told me that Alice was the daughter of one of her American friends and that she wanted her to enjoy her last night in Kabul before heading out to India.

I invited Alice to join my guests at my table. Jamila had another engagement, so she left.

As it turned out, Alice came from a well-to-do family from Atlanta, Georgia. Her father was involved in the oil business, and after Alice graduated from college her grandmother had given her an around-the-world trip as a graduation present.

When I found out that she had arrived in Kabul only two days before, I insisted that she stay a while longer to see some beautiful parts of my Afghanistan. I even suggested that if she stayed I would accompany her to some exotic parts of the country. She agreed without hesitation and said that she would send a telegram to her parents the next day, informing them of her decision. That evening I took her to the InterContinental hotel, where she was staying, and promised that I would pick her up the next day to start our sightseeing tour.

Arriving at the hotel bright and early, I found Alice waiting for me in the lobby. She told me that she had already sent a telegram to her parents stating that she was cancelling the rest of her trip.

The bellhop put her luggage in my Land Rover and we happily set off on our adventure. Accompanied by my driver, Ghulam, our first trip was to Mazar e Sharif, a historic city dating back several centuries. We traveled north through winding roads to the highest tunnel in the world, the Salang Pass. Built by Soviet engineers in the 1960s, it penetrated the Hidukush Mountains at almost 4000 meters, or 2.5 miles. The tunnel was three kilometers, or almost two miles long.

Alice was like a child in a candy store, totally elated. Her eyes were full of wonder as we passed the nomadic tribes walking alongside their camel caravans, loaded with their tents and other belongings, heading south, as was their tradition, to the warmer climates. The mountaintops were still covered with last year's snow, and down below the Salang River roared down the winding gorges, slithering like a snake. We passed by villages with houses perched high on the mountains.

Five hours after leaving Kabul we arrived in Mazar. During the journey, Alice and I exchanged information about each other's families and our lives.

When we entered the textile club in Mazar we were greeted by a prominent tribal leader named Nazekmeer, whom I had called before our departure from Kabul to tell him about our trip. Nazekmeer was a powerful Uzbak leader and owned several thoroughbred horses that competed in the great game of Buzkashi. In this game, a rider, called a Chapandaz, carries the carcass of a calf by one hand from a starting circle, down a field the size of two American football fields. He rides around a flagpole and then back to his own team's circle, and all the while other riders try to wrest the animal away from him. In the far-off past, the officers of Genghis Khan's armies played this game. Back then, however, they did not use a calf, but instead an enemy whom they had captured. The horses used in Buzkashi like the ones Nazekmeer owned were bought and sold for several hundred thousand dollars and the Chapandazes were highly paid and revered.

Nazekmeer had prepared dinner for us at his residence. While we were waiting for our ride to arrive, we met an English gentleman by the name of James. He had come to Mazar to inspect the city's cotton gin factory. Since he was alone, I invited him to join us for dinner. He gladly accepted the invitation and accompanied Alice and I to Nazekmeer's home.

Our host, dressed in an olive green silk robe worn over his long white silk shirt and baggy pants, greeted us at the gate. On his head he wore a *Karakul*, a hat made from the finest sheep's pelt.

We were led inside a large living room covered wall to wall with the most expensive Afghan Mauri carpets. Long silk curtains hang from the floor to ceiling windows and a large screen television was airing a Russian program from across the border from Uzbekistan. After being seated, Nazekmeer turned off the TV and clapped his hands, and soon a band of musicians entered the room. After seating themselves on the cushions in the far corner of the room, they began to play. Although the music was unfamiliar to both my guests, they appeared to enjoy it thoroughly. Our host again clapped his hands and in walked two male servants, one carrying a tray of glasses and another a tray of Russian Stolichnaya vodka and juices.

Since I had made it a point never to drink in public, I settled for an orange juice, as did Alice. But James went straight for the vodka and had two shots one after another. When he asked for a third, Nazekmeer asked me to tell James that he should be careful or he will get too drunk to enjoy the meal.

When I translated Nazekmeer's warning, James laughed and said that as an Englishman he could drink anyone under the table. Our host picked up the challenge and asked for two additional bottles of vodka.

By the time they had finished the first bottle, James was slurring his words. When they got through half of the second bottle, James fell sideways on the couch and was snoring in no time. Nazekmeer smiled and continued to drink without showing an inkling of being drunk. It was as though he was drinking water all night.

Sitting next to me, Alice nudged my arm and, leaning over slightly, thanked me for convincing her to stay. I whispered to her to wait until the end of our excursion before thanking me. She squeezed my arm quickly, but not before Nazekmeer had seen her affectionate gesture towards me. He told me in Pashto that she was really beautiful and wanted to know if I was going to marry her. I told him that she was my guest for a few days and was going back to the US. He nodded knowingly without uttering a word, as if to say he didn't believe it.

After a sumptuous dinner of rice, stews, and various types of kebobs, which were served according to custom on a large *destrehan*, or tablecloth, laid on the floor, I thanked our host for his generous hospitality. Alice and I followed the two guards who carried a moaning James to the car, and left for the club. We promised Nazekmeer that we would meet him in the morning as he wanted to take us to his stables to see his prized Buzkashi horses.

////////////

Having spent a restful night, I walked over to Alice's room and she opened the door on the first knock, as though she was standing behind the door waiting for me. She greeted me with a broad smile and wished me good morning in her sultry Southern accent. She wore jeans and a dark blue vest over a pale blue shirt, and her long auburn hair was tied with a bow in the back of her head. We walked down to the club restaurant where waiters were waiting to serve us breakfast. As soon as we finished eating, the manager of the club came in to tell me that Nazekmeer was waiting for us outside. As we walked out we ran into James, who did not look very well. I laughed at his composure and told him that he should never challenge an Afghan to drink. He mumbled something as he held his head and walked toward the dining room to drown his pain in a hot cup of tea.

Outside, Nazekmeer greeted us as he opened the back door of his Mercedes. Alice and I got in the back seat while he sat in the front with the driver. We drove out of the city to the green fields where Nazekmeer kept his horses in specially built stables. When we arrived there, Nazekmeer called out to one of the stable boys and soon we saw the boy come out of the stable holding a magnificent, shiny black stallion by the reins. The horse kept moving from side to side, neighing. Alice stood there with her mouth wide open, admiring the beautiful creature.

When the boy reached us, Alice walked up to the horse and began to caress its neck and mutter soft words that only the horse could hear. I was amazed at the effect she had on the horse. While a few minutes earlier he appeared wild and agitated, now with Alice's touch and words, he became as calm as a kitten.

Nazekmeer was highly impressed by her action and told her that if she would like to ride the horse, he would saddle it for her. She smiled and said she did not need a saddle as she had been riding horses since childhood and had one of her own back home. She grabbed the reins from the boy and with one swing of her long legs straddled the horse and took off like the wind down the field.

Nazekmeer smiled at me and said that a prince should marry such a woman. I did not say anything. I was too busy about other things to think about marriage, especially to someone I had just met.

After a short while and a full gallop down the field, Alice returned and brought the horse to a halt just before us. Her cheeks were flushed from the wind and as she got off she kissed the stallion on the cheek. As she handed the reins to the boy, she thanked our host for the unforgettable pleasure of riding such a fine animal.

Nazekmeer took the reins from the boy and told Alice that it was indeed his honor that Prince Ali had brought her to his humble abode. He further added that so Alice would not forget Mazar and Afghanistan, he was presenting the horse to her as a gift.

You could have knocked Alice over with a straw. Her eyes and mouth were wide open and she could not speak. Finally, she squealed and threw her arms around Nazekmeer's shoulders, thanking him continuously. Our host was slightly taken aback, as women are not allowed to show affection in public. Clearing his throat, he shook her hand and said that she must decide what to do with the horse. She said that the horse was happy being where he was and that she would definitely be back to ride him again and again. I was busy thinking about other things to take notice of her statement, but Nazekmeer had not missed a beat. When we got back to the club and were saying our goodbyes, Nazekmeer whispered in my ear that even though I had not made up my mind about marriage, Alice already had.

Without responding to him, I hugged him three times, pressing my chest against his, once to the right, once to the left and the once again to the right, as was our custom, and thanked him for his generous hospitality. He kissed my hand and had a handshake with Alice, wishing her a safe journey and inviting her to visit Mazar as often as she wished.

Since we still had time before we continued on our journey, I suggested a visit to the famous Blue Mosque where, according to legend, Ali, the son-in-law of Prophet Mohammad (PBUH), was buried. The mosque, covered with blue and white tiles, was a work of mosaic art, unlike any structure in the world.

When we arrived there, I suggested to Alice that she should put a scarf on her head as we were entering a very important Shiite religious shrine. When we got to the entrance, we had to remove our shoes and walk on pure white marble tiles. The courtyard was covered with fluttering white pigeons. Amazingly, only the white pigeons came to the shrine. None of the grey pigeons, which flew around the mosque, landed in the courtyard. Alice had noticed this and when she asked me why, I had no answer.

I gave Alice some afghanis to give to the beggars who were milling around us. She happily accepted my offer and doled out the money, mostly to the women beggars who were cuddling babies.

Since foreign women were not allowed to go inside the mosque, we walked around the shrine and then made our way back to the car, which my driver had kept running in case we had to make a hasty retreat due to the mobs that had gathered around this beautiful *Kharejai* who was handing out money.

Leaving Mazar behind, we left for Kabul. On the way to Mazar I drove and Alice sat in the passenger seat in the front. Going back to Kabul, however, I told the driver to drive and we got in the back seat. The driver held the door open while Alice got in and I followed. As soon as the door was closed, Alice slid over to my side and sat very close to me. As we were driving through the Salang Valley, I felt her hand slowly slide over my hand, which was resting on the seat. I did not move my hand as I turned to look at her. She smiled and squeezed my hand and whispered that she had never in her life had such an experience. Then she once again thanked me for making her stay.

By the time we got to Kabul it was too late to start the second half of our journey, a visit to the historical city of Herat, situated in the southeastern part of Afghanistan, bordering Iran. It was a much longer trip than to Mazar-e-Sharif. I dropped Alice off at her hotel and drove home. On the way to my house, I stopped at the club to check things out. Majid, my new manager, assured me that business was very good and that everything was under control.

Early the next morning I picked up Alice and we drove to the airport to catch a flight to Herat. Since driving time to Herat was over ten hours, mostly through barren deserts, flying there was more convenient and quick.

We flew on the national airline, Bakhtar Air. The flight took about two hours. Since I had called ahead, a car was waiting for us on the tarmac. Some tribal elders had come to the airport to greet me. They were surprised to see me walk down the steps followed by a foreign lady. I quickly made up a story that the *khanum sahib*, or lady, was the daughter of an important American businessman and that she was doing research on conducting investment in Afghanistan. Seeing that Herat, besides its history, was an industrial city with many prominent entrepreneurs, they believed me and were happy to welcome her.

Since we were flying back to Kabul that afternoon, I bid farewell to the elders and drove off to visit as many sites as we could within the short time that we had. The driver took us to the Citadel, the ancient fort on top of a hill overlooking the entire city. Then we visited the famous Blue Mosque and afterward had time for Alice to walk around the bazaar and shop for some of the blue glass pottery that Herat was famous for.

Next we visited the mausoleum of a saint known as *Khoja Ghaltan e Wali*, "the rolling saint." Legend had it that the *Khoja* was returning from a battle and when he reached the outskirts of the city, he had a vision of the entire land being covered by the bodies of dead soldiers. Not wanting to degrade their bodies by walking over them, he lay down and rolled over their bodies. He finally died while rolling over the multitude of bodies and was buried in the exact spot where he had lost his life.

The mausoleum was a walled compound with the grave of the saint situated on an upper level. Below that was an area of flat, smooth ground. When we were ushered inside the compound by the holy man who guarded the mausoleum, we were asked if we wanted to experience what the saint had experienced while rolling. I was not too sure about his offer, but Alice insisted that she try it. Leading Alice to the base of the mound of the grave, he asked her to lie down flat and cover her eyes with her hands. She did as was told. The holy man put two fingers under her shoulder and gave her a boost. To my amazement, Alice started rolling very fast towards the end of the courtyard. Before hitting the wall, the holy man ran and stopped her.

Alice got up with a look of total confusion. I asked her if she was all right. She said that she was, but could not believe what had taken place. While rolling, she had tried as hard as she could to remove her hands from eyes, but could not. It was as though her hands were attached to her face.

I figured that the ground must have a slight tilt and she had rolled downhill. In order to disprove her experience, I decided to try it myself. I lay down, put my hands on my face, and told the holy man that I was ready. He put his two fingers under my shoulders and gave me a gentle boost. I started rolling, slowly at first, and then picking up speed. I tried to uncover my eyes, but I could not. My motion was out of my control. Finally, I felt the hands of the old man stopping me. I got up, convinced that I had rolled down a hill, but to my surprise, I noticed that I had ended up where I had started from. In other words, I had rolled down the courtyard and had made a U-turn and rolled back to the mound. The old man smiled at my confused look and asked me if I had changed my mind about the power of the saint. Mumbling in agreement, I pulled out a wad of several thousand afghanis and stuffed it in his scraggy hand, wishing him well.

As soon as Alice and I got in the car, she could not hold back her astonishment. I must admit, I too was amazed at what had transpired. I told her that Afghanistan was full of legends and places like the one we had experienced. I could tell by the look on her face that Alice was becoming enthralled by her Afghanistan journey. She had a look of childlike wonder and glee on her face.

When we settled into our seats on the plane, Alice hooked her arm in mine and looked directly into my eyes. She said that Afghanistan was a place where she could spend the rest of her life. I responded that perhaps some lucky Afghan could win her heart and fulfill her dream. She squeezed my arm and said that she already had found such a person. Without hesitation, she asked me if I would marry her. The suddenness of her proposal left me dumbfounded. For a moment, I was speechless. Looking at her beautiful face and feeling her warmth next to me, I said that we should discuss the matter when we got back to Kabul. I wanted her to be absolutely certain about the major decision that she was making. She squeezed my arm once again and put her head on my shoulder for the rest of the trip back to Kabul.

When I dropped her off at the hotel, she invited me to her room. The moment we were inside she threw her arms around my neck and kissed me passionately. After our long kiss, she looked into my eyes and said that I had made her the happiest girl in the world. She said that she never thought that her grandmother's graduation gift would include a husband. She let go of me and twirled around the room, singing that she was getting married.

Things were moving so fast that I did not even have time to think things through. All I could think of was that this beautiful Southern girl from the United States had woven her magic around me. Granted, I was getting bored with my daily routine and missed not having a permanent relationship that entailed love and partnership. But was Alice the one? Well, I thought, why not? All others came, stayed, and then left, leaving an emptiness in their place. But Alice was different. She thought of me as me, not as a prince, or a club owner, or rich. She wanted me for me and for Afghanistan. The whole idea appealed to me and I took her in my arms. After giving her a kiss, I said that I would be proud to have her as my wife.

The next morning, I took Alice to the airport so she could catch her flight to the US. She told me that she would call me as soon as she discussed our forthcoming marriage with her parents.

I returned to the club, went to the bar, and even though it was not yet cocktail hour, I had Rashid fix me a stiff Scotch on the rocks. I took my drink to my office, plopped myself down on my stuffy chair, and took a swig. I reflected on the details of what had transpired over the last few days, and when I arrived at my agreeing to get married, I nearly choked on my drink. MARRIED?

I had been down that road before, so long ago that I had completely put the experience out of my mind. I had been a child groom married to an equally young woman, a double first cousin, in fact, and the marriage did not last more than eighteen months. So much had happened in my life since then that I barely believed that I had once been married.

But this was going to be different. This was going to involve the unification of two cultures. I realized that I was trying to create excuses for having made this most serious decision for my life. Had I been too hasty? Nah! It was going to be a great new experience for me.

Convincing myself of my decision, I walked out of my office and went to see Safia. When I told her about what I had done, she laughed out loud and congratulated me with a big hug. I asked her if I was not rushing into it. She said that Alice seemed like a very nice young lady and that she would fit perfectly with our plans to set up an Afghanistan center in Paris.

Safia's reaction was a welcome relief. I kissed her and said that I was looking forward to Paris. Soon thereafter, Safia left for Paris and I got engrossed in my work. As more days passed, I realized that I was thinking less and less of Alice.

My cousin Salah was not as forthcoming. He told me that I was being too hasty and that I should remember the first time I got married. They had all warned me not to move too quickly, and Salah reminded me that I did not listen. He asked me what, if anything, I knew about her or her family He warned me not to do something crazy just because I was bored.

Even though I knew in my heart that Salah was right, my mind was made up. I told him that I was not bored, but just fed up with everything. My life was empty and lonely.

He shook his head and said that he hoped that I would not end up regretting my decision.

The first week of December 1972, I got a telegram from Alice asking me to call her. In those days, international calls had to be booked ahead of time, so I scheduled my call and finally got Alice on the line. She told me that her father was very interested in meeting me. Since he had business trips to New York often, could I please come to New York? She further told me that she had decided to wait until her parents met me to tell them about our impending marriage.

Since I had plans to go to Paris to see Safia anyway, I told her that once in Paris, I would let her know when I would be in New York. We ended the call with many expressions of "I love you" and promises that we would see each other soon. I could not leave before the New Year, as the club was fully booked for the New Year Eve's party, but she understood.

The weeks went by quickly, and on New Year's Eve the club was packed to the limit. The band was playing hard rock and people were dancing to the rhythm of the pulsating dance floor lights. A long-time friend, Lee Anne, showed up at the club with my good friend and cousin Timmy Hamid. I had known Lee Anne for years as her father was an executive of Pan Am airlines, and I was very interested in her. I would have liked to have had a deeper relationship with her, but unfortunately, outside of a stolen kiss in the dining room of her house, I did not get any encouragement to carry the relationship further. A beautiful blonde, Lee Anne looked stunning as she and Timmy joined me at my table.

Everyone was happy. At midnight the lights came up, the band broke into "Auld Lange Syne," and streamers and balloons fell from the ceiling. The guests hugged their partners and burst into wishing each other Happy New Year. Looking around, I felt a sense of emptiness. I stood up from the table, wished Lee Anne and Timmy a Happy New Year, and walked out of the club. I went directly home and started to pack my suitcase.

The following day, I boarded the plane and flew to Paris.

Ahead of my arrival I had rented an apartment on Avenue Kleber near the Champs Élysées. After dropping my suitcase at the apartment, I went to see Safia who lived on Avenue Henry Martin, a very high-society neighborhood. She was very happy to see me and after having coffee in her luxurious house, we got in her Rolls Royce and drove to the George V Hotel to see the future location of the Afghanistan Centre.

Baron Philippe's building was located directly across from the hotel. We walked in and examined the available space and found it very suitable for our venture. As the Baron was out of the country, we decided to wait until his return. Since we had time on our hands, Princess Safia decided to go to Zermatt, Switzerland, for skiing and I decided to fly to New York to meet Alice's father.

///////////

NEW YORK, NEW YORK

It was a damp and chilly afternoon when I walked up Park Avenue to Alice's parents' apartment. Alice was more certain than ever that her parents would share her excitement when they met me and learned that we were getting married.

A stiffly pompous servant answered the door, took my coat and gloves, and led me through the foyer and into the salon. The apartment was luxuriously decorated with wall-to-wall carpeting and geometric furniture in muted tones. I supposed they thought it to be GQ, but to me it was as drab as drab could be. I glanced at the unsmiling faces on the pewter-framed family photographs that sat on the coffee table.

Alice's gleeful voice called out to me from the hallway, and when she bounded into the room she threw her arms around my neck and kissed me full on the mouth. I lifted her and cradled her in my arms.

I told her I missed her, trying very hard not to sound mechanical. The truth was I had not really missed her. Our time apart had made me think twice about what I was about to commit to, and Salah's warnings kept ringing in my ear. Still, I was here and wanted to see how everything was going to play out. It was the first time I was going to meet my future in-laws and I wanted to make a good impression. The discomfort I felt in my stuffy grey suit matched the conflicting thoughts clattering around in my mind.

Alice whispered that "Mummy and Daddy" would join us in a minute. She said that she had told them all about me, and they did not suspect a thing. She was sure they would be so happy when they heard the news. I suddenly felt like a thoroughbred horse on display, about to be examined by potential buyers. I had never been in such a position in my life, but I played along.

No wonder, I thought, looking around the painfully colorless room, Alice had decided to settle in exotic Afghanistan as my wife. My thoughts were disrupted with the gruff greeting of "Howdy, partner," from behind me. I looked over my shoulder and beheld a rugged, bow-legged man in his late fifties wearing a cowboy hat.

I put Alice down gently and walked over to shake her father's hand.

Mr. McCarey then introduced me to a slight woman with bleached hair and a pale complexion standing a step behind him. Mrs. McCarey extended a frail manicured hand and greeted me with a heavy Texas drawl. I kissed the back of her hand.

The cowboy looked me up and down and said with a chuckle that it was good to meet the boy who had stolen their baby girl's heart. The Texan's attitude was beginning to get on my nerves. Especially when he asked where I was from. I told him that I was from Afghanistan. To be polite, I added "sir" at the end of my statement.

"Afghanistan," Mrs. McCarey said, sounding surprised. She asked me if that was somewhere near Brazil. I told her as politely as I could that it was somewhere near India. My answer confused her even more.

Mr. McCarey apologized for his wife's lack of knowledge of geography and invited me to sit down. Alice's mother continued by telling me that I did not look like an Indian. She thought that Indians were darkies that wore big turbans and worshipped cows. She wanted to know if "Afghanistanis" worshipped cows.

By now I was losing my patience with her questioning and I curtly replied that the people of my country were known as Afghans and that we were Muslims and worshiped one God, Allah.

Then the cowboy joined in half jokingly with a comment about Muslim men being able to marry four wives. I had had enough. My patience was gone and I could not control myself. I proudly informed the cowboy and his wife that my grandfather, King Habibullah, had 36 wives. The woman gasped and took a deep gulp of whatever she was drinking.

"Is that true?" she asked.

"Yes, Mrs. McCary," I said, "and not only did my grandfather marry thirty-six wives, but he also sired sixty-two children." She gasped again and covered her mouth with her hand.

Before she could recover, Alice interrupted and hastily declared that she was going to marry me. I heard a loud THUMP from across the room and quickly looked over to see that Mrs. McCarty had fainted and dropped to the floor. Mr. McCarty crouched down beside her and held her hand.

"Mummy!" Alice screeched.

An army of servants rushed into the salon and attempted to awaken their mistress. Her father took off his hat and began fanning her face.

He began to explain to me that his wife was affected by the heat and then asked one of the maids to carry his wife to her bedroom. He gestured for Alice to attend to her mother. Then he turned to me and asked me to take a seat.

I sat on the beige sofa and watched a servant come in with a silver tray. He set a coaster on the coffee table, followed by a glass of orange juice.

Mr. McCary repeated that it must have been the heat, unmindful of the fact that it was the dead of winter. Then he said that maybe it was the shock of Alice's announcement of marriage. He asked me if I intended to take their Alice to Afghaniland."

"Afghanistan," I corrected him.

He apologized and corrected himself.

By then I had heard and seen enough to realize that it was not going to work between Alice and me. Salah was right. I had not known anything about this family. But some unruly impulse compelled me to keep up the charade.

I said that as my wife, Alice would be expected to live with me in my country. He looked disdainful. He said that Afghanistan was so far away and asked me to reconsider. This sentiment didn't surprise me, but nothing could have prepared me for what he said next. He offered to pay me, buy me an apartment in New York City, and give me a high position within his company if I only agreed to stay in the United States and not take their little Alice so far away.

I was totally dumbfounded. Instead of appreciating that his daughter was about to be brought into an illustrious royal family, he was implying that I was a gigolo after Alice for her money. In a calm, cool voice I asked him how much money he had in the bank. His face went white and he started to stutter. Without waiting for his answer, I told him that whether he had millions or billions, he could take that money and multiply that by one hundred, and it still would not amount to what had gone into making me what I am. I told him that I had a thousand years of history flowing through my veins with twelve kings of Afghanistan as my ancestors. I told him to marry his daughter off to some other man whom he could buy for her. As I got up to leave, I heard him say that he now realized why his Alice had fallen in love with me. That I was a determined young man who spoke his mind.

And so it was that I left the McCarey's Park Avenue apartment without as much as bidding Alice goodbye. I wanted to spare her the embarrassment of her parents' behavior.

Once outside, I felt as if a huge weight had been lifted off my shoulders. I walked quickly, like a man who had just escaped the guillotine. I stepped into the nearest bar, ordered a Scotch, and called my friend Ira Seret who had moved from Afghanistan to New York.

CHAPTER 8

DOORWAY TO LOVE

As it happened, Ira had just returned from Afghanistan and was very happy to hear my voice. He invited me to check out of my hotel and stay with him for as long as I wanted. I took him up on his offer and showed up at his apartment door that afternoon.

Ira lived in an elegant old building directly across from Gracie Mansion on Manhattan's Upper East Side. He had brought a taste of home to his décor by covering the wall around the huge fireplace with raw lapis lazuli, a semi-precious stone from Afghanistan. To prepare for my stay, he had erected a tent in the middle of the huge living room, covered with multicolored mattresses and cushions in typical Afghan village style. That was my sleeping area.

One evening, while I was telling Ira about my life as a student in Connecticut, my thoughts rolled back to my encounter with the beautiful Maribeth Blawie, and I wondered what had happened to her and her sister Pam. Since my last meeting with her, my life had gone through so many turns with so many people that I had completely forgotten my prediction about Maribeth's future. After Ira and I finished visiting, I picked up the phone and called Pam's number, which I still had in my black book. A sweet voice answered the phone and when I introduced myself, the first words out of her lips were, "Oh, my God!" Then she told me that Pam was not there and that she was Beth, her younger sister. I told her that in fact I was calling to reach her, not Pam, and that I was in New York and hoped to see her. I asked her for her address. At first she was reluctant, but she finally gave in and told me that she lived in Greenwich Village and gave me the address. As soon as I hung up, I put on my long, high-collared, green Count Monte Cristo coat, tied an ascot around my neck, and grabbed a taxi to see my future wife.

When Maribeth greeted me at the door her deep blue eyes looked me up and down and the smile on her face assured me that she approved of what she saw. We walked into the living room and she sat across from me. She talked about her trip to Europe and meeting my sister. I told her about Afghanistan and my family and about life in Kabul. The more I talked, the more intrigued she became. I could almost feel the excitement that my stories were building in her. I insisted that she visit Afghanistan. As I was talking, I heard the apartment door open and Pam's voice. She entered the room followed by a bespectacled gentleman whom she introduced as Arthur Woodstone. Arthur was a journalist and author who had just released his book, *Nixon's Head*.

We continued talking into the wee hours of the night, eating the pizza Pam had brought. We all met up again the following night for dinner at a popular restaurant in the village, and as soon as we arrived a woman walked to our table carrying an armful of roses. I bought the entire bouquet and placed it in front of Maribeth. She glanced at the flowers and without saying anything, and pushed them to one side. I thought that she did that in order not to block the view. I was wrong. After we finished and I paid the bill, we all got up to go and Maribeth left the roses on the table without a glance. I thought her action was very strange, but I did not make an issue of it.

Before calling it a night, Arthur invited us to a Greek restaurant where they had belly dancing, and we spent another hour there. Back out on the sidewalk, Maribeth tucked her arm in mine as we crossed the street. Without looking at her, I told her to be ready at eight the following night, as I was going to take her out to dinner. She looked up at me and said, "Don't you believe in asking if I want to go out with you?" I told her jokingly that anyone who would leave a beautiful gift of flowers behind without even saying thank you need not be asked. She apologized and said that she thought I had bought the flowers for the table and not particularly for her. She squeezed my arm tighter and leaned her head against my shoulder as we walked to her apartment. Pam and Arthur had gone on to Arthur's apartment. Since it was late, Maribeth asked me if I wanted to spend the night at her place. I readily accepted, as I did not want the evening to end. When we arrived at the apartment, she gave two choices of where I could sleep: on the small couch in the living room or on the floor in her bedroom. I chose the floor in her bedroom. She threw me a sheet and a pillow and I happily spent the night on the concrete floor. I didn't care, as long as I was close to her.

The next day I made a reservation at Thursdays, a popular restaurant behind the Plaza Hotel, and picked her up at eight in a rented limousine. As soon as we were seated I ordered a bottle of Dom Perignon, and Maribeth looked at me with a smile of approval. She loved champagne, she said. When the waiter returned I ordered two of the best steaks on the menu, but Maribeth cleared her throat and apologetically informed me that she was a vegetarian. We did not find any vegetarian dishes on the menu, but the waiter came to the rescue by suggesting an omelet with vegetables. She happily accepted his suggestion. I could not gorge myself on a dead animal in front of her, of course, so I changed my order to an omelet too. Before our meal arrived, we sipped on the Dom Perignon and enjoyed the chocolate-covered strawberries that the waiter had brought as a compliment of the house. On the drive home Maribeth invited me to accompany her to Fairfield, Connecticut, the next day to meet her parents and family over the weekend. I spent another night on the hard floor, and early the next morning we stopped by Ira's apartment to pick up some clothes before heading to Grand Central Station to catch a train to Fairfield.

Maribeth's younger brother Paul picked us up at the station in his father's Cadillac convertible. As we drove along the wooded lanes, Maribeth told me that her father loved tennis and would surely challenge me to a game. She confided that he hated losing, but I just nodded my head and continued enjoying the scenic ride. Soon the car turned into another lane and I saw my first glimpse of the charming Blawie mansion.

Once inside, Maribeth introduced me to the Blawie clan. Even though I had casually met them when I was last there, this was a formal visit and Maribeth wanted them to know that I was her guest. As soon as I sat down in the living room, Mr. Blawie walked over and asked what size shoes I wore. I told him size 12. He left and soon enough returned with a pair of sneakers and a tennis racquet and asked me to follow him to the tennis court for a friendly game.

When we started to play, I forgot Maribeth's warning of how her father hated to lose and played my best game ever. I won the first set, and to Mr. Blawie's chagrin, the second as well. Refusing to play a third set, Mr. Blawie headed back to the house.

After a hot shower, I joined the group in the family room. Everyone, except for Maribeth, gathered around me, asking me questions about Afghanistan, Afghan royalty, and life in my country. After about a half hour Maribeth grabbed me by the hand and in a cold and stern voice practically ordered me to come with her.

I followed her out to the garden and past the gate to a horse farm next door to her residence. We did not speak a word until we stopped by an old tree. She turned around and kissed me and said that she was tired of sharing everything with the entire family. She told me that she had brought me home to meet her family, not to share me with them. I was hers and not theirs. I was totally taken aback by her reaction and extremely happy to hear her express her feelings for me. I held her tight in my arms and told her that no one was ever going to take me away from her. I knew there and then that she was mine for life.

When we got back to the house, the family was involved in a game of charades. Pam and Arthur had also arrived from New York and we all joined in the game. Later, we switched to bridge, and I learned that the Blawies had reached the Master's level in the game. As I sat down to play with Pam and two other sisters, Paula, the recently married fourth daughter, stopped at our table to be introduced to me. Before she left, I asked her to please bring me a glass of water. She turned around and without missing a beat told me to get my own water. I was quite surprised by her reaction because I was used to people doing what I asked them to do. Well this was America, and I had a few things to learn. So I went and got my own water.

When it was time to go to bed, Maribeth walked me towards the room that had been prepared for me. When we got there, we found her father fast asleep on the bed. Apparently, some of the younger kids had crawled into bed with Mrs. Blawie in the master bedroom, not leaving any place for Mr. Blawie. He had simply found the nearest empty bed and gone to sleep. Maribeth was very apologetic about the situation, but I told her not to worry. Having spent two nights on her hard concrete floor, any soft place would do. We found me a nice long couch down in the playroom, and after bringing me pillows and a blanket, Maribeth kissed me good night and went up to her room.

The next morning after breakfast, Pam said that her mother wanted to know about my intentions for Maribeth. Without any hesitation, I told her that I intended to marry her.

///////////

Shortly after meeting the Blawie family I returned home to Afghanistan, and Maribeth joined me, as she promised she would, a few months later in March of 1973. As we drove to my house in the section of the city called Wazir Akbar Khan, named after my grand-uncle, I thought about the confrontations I had had with some of my relatives over the past few weeks. Maribeth would never know about their protests about my marrying a foreigner, I would make sure of that. I did not want anything to stand in the way of her having an unforgettable introduction to my family, my city, and my country. We made our way through Kabul to my two-story, four-bedroom house that for three years had served as the perfect hideout for a bachelor prince.

As soon as we got home, Beth went into her private bath to take a shower. Coming out of the bathroom, draped in a white robe with her hair flowing down around her shoulders, she looked breathlessly beautiful. As she entered the bedroom, I could not wait any longer. I went to the safe and pulled out a small box that contained a 50-carat topaz, set in gold. I took her hand in mine, and putting the ring on her finger, asked her to marry me. I said that until I exchanged the ring for a diamond, this ring would serve as an engagement ring. She smiled and said that the reason she had traveled halfway around the globe to come to me was because she had already made up her mind that she was going to be my wife. I grabbed her in my arms and kissed her.

We were engaged against the wishes of my parents and my father's sisters, who were the most adamant about their misgivings. They came over to our house once again and told my father and me privately that they did not want the royal blood of the family to be mingled with that of a foreign woman. I told them that the decision did not lie with my father, but with me. Furthermore, I continued with a smile, it would do the family good to bring in fresh new blood. They walked out with a look of disdain on their faces.

Once my parents accepted the fact that I was not going to change my mind, my mother invited Beth for lunch the next day. At my parents' house, my mother ruled. Every aspect of life within the residence was based on a tight schedule. Breakfast was at 9:00 a.m., lunch at 12:00 noon. High tea was served at 6:00 p.m. sharp and dinner began at 9:00. There was no deviation from these times, so at noon the next day Beth and I were seated in our places in the dining room. At our house, my mother would sit at the head of the table, my father to her left, the guest on her right, and others in the remaining chairs. The servants brought out the food and set each item in its appropriate place—the rice in front of my mother, the stews and other dishes in various locations on the table.

In Afghan tradition a dish called *kala pacha* is served on special occasions, such as when honoring a guest. This meal consisted of the feet, stomach, and head of a sheep all baked under a pile of rice sautéed in crystallized onions and topped with red raisins and shredded carrots. My mother had such a meal prepared in honor of my wife-to-be. As the servants stepped in with the platter piled high with rice it completely slipped my mind to forewarn my mother about Beth being a vegetarian. Before I could say anything, my mother, following her custom of serving everyone, began piling a ladle full of rice on Beth's plate. Everyone who knew my mother knew that when one said please stop, no more, she automatically dished out three times more. So when I told my mother that that was enough rice for Beth, she scooped up three more helpings and exposed the head of the sheep. As if this was not bad enough, the sheep's eyes were staring straight at Beth. Now, it is customary in our society that the guest of honor gets the eyes of the sheep. Therefore, my father, living up to the tradition, plucked out one of the eyes and gently placed it on the pile of rice on Beth's plate, with the pupil looking directly at her. I had never in my life seen blood drain so quickly from someone's face. Maribeth was frozen, her mouth agape and big blue eyes fixated on the eyeball on her plate. I swept up her plate and gave it to a servant, and then respectfully informed my parents that Maribeth was a vegetarian.

My mother apologized and chastised me for not informing her ahead of time. Fortunately, the issue was resolved before the head of the sheep could be cracked open to pull the brain out to be served to the diners—as was also the custom. My mother then served Beth white rice with one of the meatless stews and the sheep head was sent out to the servant quarters for the help to enjoy. I could see the disappointment in my father's face, for he loved *kala pacha*, but out of respect for the guest, he did not object.

We proceeded to enjoy a wonderful lunch talking over our wedding plans. Maribeth and I had decided to get married in the US, as I was planning on going back to get my master's degree in international business. That was the plan. But the political upheavals that followed soon thereafter blew those plans apart.

//////////

On the morning of July 14, 1973, I got a frantic call from the club manager informing me that government officials had arrived to close down the club. I quickly got dressed and drove over, and a group of officials from the Security Division met me at the door. A man named Said Jamal handed me a government petition stating that they had come to search the premises for alcoholic beverages.

Luckily, every night after I closed the club I locked up most of the bottles in a locker in the back of my office to prevent them from being stolen. Except for a few liqueurs, the bar was clean. They confiscated those and said that the government had ordered all clubs and bars to be closed until further notice. They locked up the club with a padlock and left as quickly as they came.

Down the road, they did the same to Marco Polo and other clubs. I was confused by this action, but decided to give it a few days before approaching the government to find out what was going on.

//////////

JULY 16, 1973

The moon was full that summer night. Maribeth, who had been with me for four joyful months, was sleeping peacefully next to me. The next three bedrooms were occupied by my friend and fraternity brother, Michael Jones, and his wife and three boys. Mike, who worked for a major US oil company, had come to Kabul to sign an oil exploration contract with the Ministry of Mines and Industry. Because of my contacts in the Afghanistan government, Mike's company had entrusted him with the responsibility of landing the multi-million-dollar deal. I had set up an appointment for him with the oil minister for the next day.

The night's silence was suddenly disrupted by the rattle of machine-gun fire. I jumped out of bed, ran to the window, and asked my guard below what was going on. He told me that the sound came from across the field from my house. I ran to the closet and grabbed my rifle, and as I got to the hall outside my bedroom Mike came out of his room, looking bewildered. I told him to stay put while I checked it out. After I left the house I told the guard to lock all the doors. When I got out to the street, I saw my cousin General Nadeer Seraj standing out at his gate two doors down from me. Nazeer was the chief of logistics at the Ministry of Defense, and that night he was in full uniform with several soldiers standing next to him.

When I got to him I asked what was going on. He looked at me and said that I should first go back home and put some clothes on. I looked down and saw that I was still dressed in my skimpy underwear with bare feet and a rifle in hand. I must have made a comical sight, as I noticed the soldiers smirking beneath their moustaches.

I ran back to my house, and after getting dressed returned to my cousin. The general explained that Daoud, King Zahir Shah's cousin, had initiated a coup d'état and taken over the government.

I quickly went home and gave my rifle to Mike. I explained what I had heard and told him that I was going to drive around to see what was going on. My guard and I set out for Daoud's residence, and when we got to the area we found several tanks with soldiers sitting on the turrets. They waved to me and I to them. I followed the tank tracks past the Ministry of Foreign Affairs and the Ministry of Defense, which was located across the street from the palace, and then around the city. I realized then that the tanks must have been used in the arrests of officials and other individuals.

I returned home and gave the details to Mike, who, in his soft-spoken manner, told me that the coup must have been initiated by the Soviets, as they did not want an American company to explore for oil in Afghanistan. To this day, Mike is convinced of that.

Knowing that the coup leader was a member of our family, I stayed calm. I knew that we were safe and I assured Mike of that. At this time, my father was in Europe and my mother was alone at her house, so Beth and I left my security guard with Mike and drove over to spend the night at my mother's.

After we settled in I suddenly realized why the government had closed the clubs. It was not the government, but Daoud's supporters within the government who had planned this. Since they were going to initiate a coup, they did not want people roaming the streets at night. To prevent that, they closed the clubs under the pretext that they were serving alcohol. Certain that this was the case, I relaxed and I figured that after a few days things would go back to normal.

Back home the next morning I was happy to hear that Mike and his family had had a restful night. While we were talking, we heard the rattle of tank engines outside. Both Mike and I ran to the upstairs terrace and saw five tanks roaring around the circle on the street in front of my house. Before I could warn him not to, Mike grabbed his camera and started taking photos. When I saw one of the tanks turn its turret toward us, I quickly pulled Mike inside the house. That was a dangerous move on Mike's part, but he was very happy to have captured the photos.

The tank maneuver seemed to be the last action of the coup, so with calm returned to Kabul we took Mike and his family on a sightseeing tour of the city and the suburbs. Before leaving, I informed my guard, Philipo (so-named by a Spanish friend), that a tribal leader from the North was going to bring me a baby leopard sometime that day. I asked him to put the animal somewhere safe with a bowl of water, for the little animal may be thirsty after its long trip.

When we returned, I blew the car horn for Philipo to open the gate. After several attempts, I got out of the Jag and rang the doorbell at the gate. Finally, the door opened and I saw a bedraggled Philipo with torn sleeves and a bloody arm. I was concerned that someone had broken into the house and attacked him, but before I could ask him anything, he gasped and blubbered that there was a lion in the house. I asked him if he meant the little leopard I was expecting. He shook his head and said no, that there was a large lion in the kitchen. Trembling all over, he said that the tribal elder had delivered a lion about an hour earlier.

We dashed into the house and carefully opened the kitchen door. Philipo told me that he had pushed the lion into the large cabinet under the sink and, after covering his hand and arm with a paper bag, put a bowl of water in front of it. The animal swiped his arm with its claws. I slowly crept to the sink and opened the door a crack. Peering inside, I saw a large snow leopard hissing at me. I quickly shut the door and relocked it. The little baby leopard that I was promised some months ago was now full grown. I had forgotten that time changes everything.

Wondering what to do with this wild animal, I finally decided to call the manager of the Kabul Zoo and explain my predicament. He was ecstatic and said that the zoo would be honored to receive such a rare and endangered animal and would give the lion the utmost care and treatment. Soon thereafter, a caged van arrived and the zoo personnel managed to collar the leopard and lead him away.

///////////

Daoud's first act as a leader was to abolish the monarchy. Thus he put an end to 300 years of our joint families' inheritance and rule of Afghanistan. Soon after his ascension to power, because of inter-family enmity and my close contact with the poor and the needy, Daoud developed a very negative attitude towards me. It was no secret that I often had lunch with shopkeepers, sitting on the floor around a *desterkhan* and eating with our hands out the same ceramic bowl. While other members of my family gathered around the table at my parents' house, I often met with locals to share a meal of pigeon soup cooked in a teapot on a shop stove.

Daoud's ill feeling toward me increased when I supported the Kabul University students during their demonstrations against the Daoud government. In order to punish the students, he ordered the university canteen closed. This action against the young generation made me very angry, and I decided to deliver meals to all the students from the provinces who had to remain in the dormitories. I did this until the government reopened the canteen. Daoud regarded my actions as a direct challenge to his authority. Using the serving of alcohol at the Twenty-Five Hour Club as an excuse, he tried to imprison me for seven years without a trial. When the family found out what he had in store for me, they made loud public objections and demanded that he recant his order. He did, but he still forbade me to leave the country.

His action of closing my club so disgusted me that the day they came to reopen the club I could not bear to go inside. Daoud's action had left a sour taste in my mouth. He had driven a death nail into my creation, which had instilled such great memories in so many people, so I ordered the manager to bring in wreckers and tear the place apart.

This put a wrench in our plans to get married in the US, so in October Maribeth went back to the States to relay the news to her family. We spent the next weeks and months working out a Plan B over the phone, anxious to figure out how to begin making a life together.

While we deliberated over our new plans, I was getting itchy to start something new. My frustration over not being able to leave the country was driving me crazy, so I went out again, searching the city for a site to build another venue.

As luck would have it, I found a building undergoing new construction in the diplomatic district of Wazir Akbar Khan, right around the corner from Daoud's house. There was justice after all.

I immediately signed a contract and began building Kabul's first Chinese supper club, the Golden Lotus. Since I was not sure when I would get together with Beth again, I hired a large crew and worked around the clock, seven days a week. Three months later, construction was complete, with a Pagoda-style design, tinted-glass windows, an indoor waterfall, sunken hexagonal bar, and exterior fountains with underwater lighting.

///////////

I did not spare any expense on the place. I wanted to give Daoud the finger by building Kabul's most opulent supper club practically in his front yard. I hired a Chinese cook from Pakistan and brought my crew from The Twenty-Five Hour Club to the new establishment.

I invited the who's who of Kabul society to attend the grand opening. Guests were amazed at the grandeur and atmosphere of the place. To give life to the venue I hired a band called the Four Brothers, and following its debut the Golden Lotus was jam-packed every night. A new life was born in Kabul.

//////////

Maribeth finally returned in the summer of 1974 and we were married in a traditional Islamic ceremony in Kabul, at the Golden Lotus, with a mullah conducting the ceremony and the American Embassy Consular certifying the marriage certificate.

According to Islamic religion, a marriage cannot take place in the three months between Eidul Fitr, which marks the end of Ramadan, and Eidul Hadda (the Eid of sacrifice marking when Allah gave Abraham a sheep to sacrifice instead of his son), which marks the end of the Muslim pilgrimage to Mecca. Therefore, because it was the month of Ramadan and we did not want to wait three months, the ceremony took place in the afternoon with only the immediate family present, as no one, including employees of the restaurant, could break the fast until dusk.

According to family tradition, when a marriage took place during the day, the bride wore a green dress. Our family tailor had sewn the dress I designed for Maribeth.

On the day of the wedding, my cousin Timmy, whom both Beth and I had selected to be the best man, arrived at our house and we drove to the Golden Lotus. My parents and other guests were already there. A long table was set up in one corner for the ceremony to take place. The mullah was seated in the center, Beth and I sat opposite him, and Timmy was at my side. The mullah filled in our names on the marriage license and then asked how much I was going to put up as a dowry. Now, in traditional tribal marriages, since there is no exchange of diamond rings or, in the case of subsequent divorce, alimony, the groom's family puts up a predetermined amount of money, jewelry, and, in some cases, land and livestock. The reason behind this is that if the couple divorces or the husband dies, the wife will be taken care of. But in our family's case, we had done away with that. Instead, in order to keep up with tradition, we had put in a minimal amount of 30 afghanis as a token dowry payment, just to fill in the blank. For years thereafter, Maribeth always joked that I bought her for 30 afghanis, or 70 cents.

After the mullah completed filling in the license, he turned to me and asked if I wanted the woman sitting next to me as my wife. I accepted. Then he turned to Maribeth and asked her the same question.

Because she could not understand Dari, Timmy translated for me. When she said "Yes," the mullah put the license in front of me to sign. Then he put it in front of Beth. Since Dari is written from right to left, he pointed to the end of the line which, in Beth's mind did not leave much space for her to sign, so she tried to squeeze her signature in the small space. She made a very small signature. Then the American consul also signed, and the marriage license was officially certified.

When the document was complete, everyone clapped and, as per tradition, the waiter brought in a tray full of candies and my mother threw the candies over Maribeth's and my head. For good luck, guests close to the bride and groom always take some of the candies and either eat them or take them home. My father took one candy, unwrapped it, and asked Tim to open his mouth. My father placed the candy on his tongue. Suddenly, my father realized what he had done. This was not only the month of Ramadan, but a mullah was also sitting there looking right at him and Tim. My father quickly grabbed hold of Timmy's throat, squeezed it, and said that it was not yet the time to break the fast. Timmy opened his mouth and stuck out his tongue with the candy still sitting on it. My father grabbed the candy and gave to the waiter. The whole scene was so funny that everyone broke out in laughter.

Not long after the ceremony was over, it was time to break the fast. After dinner, Beth and I left for home, where a bottle of chilled Champagne was waiting for us.

The formal reception took place a week later, after the end of Ramadan, in the Inter-Continental Hotel. Over three hundred guests attended our black-tie reception, including the American Ambassador Theodore Eliot and Mrs. Eliot, other foreign dignitaries, members of the aristocracy, friends, and Maribeth's mother, who flew in for the wedding. Maribeth was twenty-three years old and a gorgeous bride dressed in a white chiffon dress that I had designed for her. That evening I reminded her of the prediction I had made at her house that she was going to be married before she was twenty-four years old and to a foreigner. She hugged me and said that she was very happy.

Our wedding reception should have been the happiest moment in my life, but I felt nauseated and miserable the entire day. When we got home, I went to the bathroom, and while I was brushing my teeth I noticed that the whites of my eyes were yellow. I did not mention anything to Maribeth, but early the next morning I sent Jan Ali to fetch the lab technician. When he arrived, he took one look at me and told me that I had contracted hepatitis. He immediately took a sample of my blood and left to analyze it. Maribeth was sitting on the bed looking very worried. Within an hour, the lab reports came in, confirming my fears. I assumed that I had contracted hepatitis from one of the meals I had shared with the shopkeepers—most likely the lunch I joined in a pigeon market filled with pigeon cages.

I called the family doctor, who told me that I should stay in bed for six weeks and to avoid all fats. So much for the honeymoon I had planned for us.

Late that the afternoon, Jan Ali came into our bedroom to tell me that he had brought me a specialist who was known to cure hepatitis. I gave him permission to bring the man in. Beth sat on the couch next to my bed.

There was a knock on the door and in walked this white-bearded man dressed in baggy pants and a long shirt of the local custom, wearing the traditional turban, followed by a much smaller man dressed the same way. The first man greeted me by kissing my hand and then proceeded to sit on the floor next to my bed. He asked Jan Ali for a glass bowl. When the bowl arrived, he pulled out a bottle containing an oily liquid from one pocket and a handful of what appeared to be green grass from the other. He gave the bottle and the grass to his assistant, and then proceeded to hum chants and blow on my face. He kept repeating this several times. I looked at Beth, who was observing the man's actions with wide eyes. I wondered what was going through her mind. She did not seem afraid, but amazed. I quietly whispered to her not to worry, for if the chants did not cure me, his foul breath certainly would.

After completing his chants, the man reached out and took the bowl, which the assistant had filled with the oil, and holding it in his left hand, took the bunch of green grass in his right and started stirring the oil with it. While stirring, he resumed his chanting and blowing.

His assistant stood over the chanter's head and kept saying that it was working. He told the old man to keep on stirring because the oil was turning yellow–the hepatitis was coming out of me.

I was amused at all the goings on and did not want to insult the man by telling him that the oil was yellow to begin with. When the session was finally over, he pulled an onion out of his pocket and said that I should wear it around my neck and peel off one paper-thin layer a day until all the yellow color disappeared. I thanked him and gave him a large sum of money. Bidding me farewell, he and his assistant left the room. As soon as they were gone, I ran to the bathroom to wash my face of all the long-bearded man's spit.

When I returned to bed, Beth asked me to explain what had happened and if it had worked. I laughed and said that the locals believed in such treatments. I went on to tell her that the bonesetters use raw eggs to wrap around broken bones. She smiled and named the old man the Hoochie Goochie man. I placed the onion on the bedside table and told Beth that my hepatitis would be long over before all the onion layers came off. We both laughed. It took exactly six weeks for the hepatitis to go away, the normal recovery time for the disease. More than half of the onion was still intact.

////////////

When Maribeth became pregnant, I was inducted into the military service. All Afghans were obligated to serve in the military, and with my university education and family position I was assigned to the officer's corps in the tank division. I began my six-month call of duty with a shaved head and concern for leaving Maribeth alone through the rest of her pregnancy. We decided that it would be best that she should go to the States and come back after having the baby.

The months flew by and Maribeth returned two days before my furlough with beautiful little Sahar. The moment she stepped off the plane and handed me that bundle wrapped in a pink blanket, I was the happiest man in the world. As I held Sahar in my arms, she opened her eyes and I was amazed at how large they were. She definitely had inherited the Seraj family trademark of huge, impressive eyes.

Back at the house, family members were waiting to welcome the first granddaughter of the Ghafoor Seraj dynasty. The baby's maid, who had been employed a month before her arrival, immediately scooped her out of my arms and took her to the nursery. Among the visitors were the two aunts who had rejected our marriage. They were in the living room, smiling coyly at Maribeth and me. They kissed

Beth three times on the cheeks, as was the custom, handed her a few wrapped gifts, and then went to the nursery to see Sahar.

The following day a group of tribal elders came to our house to pay their respects. According to tribal custom, this visit was for men only, so Beth stayed out of the room. As soon as they sat down and tea was served, they extended their prayers for the return of the *khanum sahib* and said they wanted to see the young prince who would keep the family name and heritage. I cleared my throat and in a firm voice told the elders that Allah in His good graces had bestowed a daughter upon me so that she may grow up to be a fine princess to help other mothers and daughters of the country. They nodded their heads in understanding and said that next time Allah would surely bestow a son to carry on the historic name of Seraj-ul-millat wa deen (Light of the Nation and Religion), the title of my grandfather, HM Amir (King) Habibullah. After this, they kissed my hand and left.

Two-and-a-half years later, when Beth was pregnant a second time and again went to the US to deliver our second child, she returned to Afghanistan with another beautiful daughter whom we named Safia. Because of the communist takeover and being practically under house arrest, I could not receive guests, especially tribal ones, so the elders did not find out about my second daughter. I often wonder what they would have said to me then.

My great-grandfather, King Amir Abdurrahman Khan,
the "Iron King," who reigned from 1880 to 1901.

My grandfather, King Habibullah Khan, who reigned from 1901 until his assassination in 1919, with two of his 29 sons. At the left is his eldest, Prince Enayatullah, and at the right is his second eldest, Prince Amanullah.

King Habibullah Khan (row two, sixth from the left) with the famous British General Lord Kitchener, to his right, among a group of British military officers in Simla, India, in 1915.

King Habibullah Khan's son, King Enayatullah Khan, and his wife, Queen Huriyta Tarzi. King Enayatullah reigned briefly in 1929.

My uncle, King Amanullah Khan, who reigned from 1919 to 1929 and led Afghanistan to independence from Britain.

The first celebration of Afghan independence, 1920, in Paghman, a resort north of Kabul.

King Amanullah and King George in London, 1928.

London welcomes King Amanullah and Queen Soraya Tarzi in 1928.

The portrait of Queen Soraya that was manipulated by British agents and distributed in Afghanistan to defame the royal family in early 1929.

*King Amanullah
and Queen Soraya.*

*The Seraj royal crest.
[PHOTO: Seraj family
archive]*

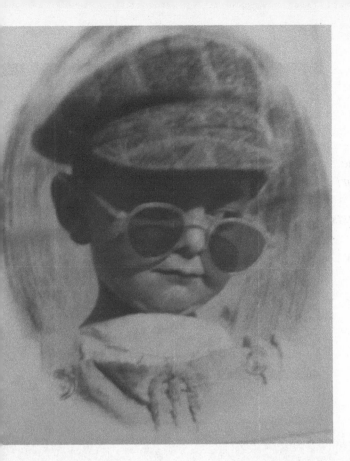

A photograph of me, age four. I did not want to have my picture taken, so my parents compromised and let me wear sunglasses. [PHOTO: Seraj family archive]

My family in 1960. Front row, left to right: My mother, Lady Siddiqa Tarzi Seraj; my father, Prince Ghafoor Seraj; and my sister, Princess Salma. Back row, left to right: my brother, Abdullah, and me. [PHOTO: Seraj family archive]

Kabul, 1974. This is the vest I would wear as part of my hippie disguise when I fled the communists on August 28, 1978. [PHOTO: Seraj family archive]

To safeguard my security when fleeing Afghanistan, the U.S. Embassy in Kabul sent this telegram to U.S. Embassy in Islamabad to issue my U.S. visa there.

Opening night of my Golden Lotus restaurant in Kabul in 1973, with Kabul Mayor Dr. Ghulam Sakhi Noorzad.
[PHOTO: Seraj family archive]

With (left to right) U.S. Ambassador William B. Taylor, King Zahir Shah, and his youngest son, Prince Mir Weis, at the royal palace in Kabul, 2006. King Zahir Shah reigned from 1933 to 1973, when he was ousted in a coup. He was in exile in Italy until 2002, when he returned to Afghanistan. The people gave him the title Father of the Nation until his death in 2007. [PHOTO: Seraj family archive]

A family in the Guzar District, north of Kabul, where I presented the woman with a house and a sheep in 2004. [PHOTO: Seraj family archive]

In the Guzar District, 2004. To my right is Don Ritter, former congressman from Pennsylvania, who was at that time the Founder and President of the Afghanistan/ America Foundation. The children are members of one family that lived in one-and one-half rooms. I built them a five-room house. [PHOTO: Seraj family archive]

A meeting of the National Coalition for Dialogue with Tribes of Afghanistan at my home in Kabul in 2008. [PHOTO: Seraj family archive]

Afghan twins who greeted me in Panjshir Province, where I provided materials for the school children in 2003. [PHOTO: Seraj family archive]

The 2010 Russia-Afghanistan Forum in Moscow, where I was the guest of honor and one of the main speakers. [PHOTO: Seraj family archive]

With my daughters, Princess Alia, in the Shawl, and Princess Safia, at the palace of Princess Elisabeth Ysenburg of Budingen, Germany, in 2008. [PHOTO. Seraj family archive]

At a formal event with my three daughters, from left to right, Princess Alia, Princess Safia, and Princess Sahar.

Me and my wife, Maribeth Blawie, 2005. [PHOTO: Seraj family archive]

On an official visit to Lahore, Pakistan, in 2008.
[PHOTO: Seraj family archive]

In Kabul in 2011. [PHOTO: Seraj family archive]

CHAPTER 9

THE GREAT ESCAPE

April 27, 1978, the fateful day that began with helicopters zooming overhead and a barrage of gunfire through our neighborhood, was a day that will haunt me for the rest of my life. We knew that President Daoud's regime was in trouble, since he had been trying to distance himself from the Soviets and was now the #1 enemy of the leader of the Afghan Communist Party, Mohammed Taraki. By the end of the day, Daoud and 18 members of his extended family had been killed, gunned down by Taraki's men in the palace, and Taraki had seized control of the country. The city was in chaos. That night, as I sat out in our courtyard, I looked up and saw my beautiful wife, with her large blue eyes, looking at me with deep concern. After putting Sahar to sleep, she had come outside to join me. She pulled a chair next to mine, held my hand, and looked straight into my eyes to ask if we were going to be all right. Hiding the gnawing feeling of danger in my soul, I soothingly told her that we would be fine. I stood up and took her in my arms, hugging her as tightly as I could. We walked inside, holding hands, both lost in thought about what lie ahead in the uncertain days to come.

The following morning my cousin and best friend, Abdullah Rafiq, came to see me. Abdullah was married to my first cousin, Mahbooba Seraj. While he was related to me through his father, he was closely related to Daoud's family, as his mother was the sister of Queen Homaira, the wife of King Zahir Shah. He bore an uncanny resemblance to President Daoud.

Abdullah's red-rimmed eyes told me that he had had a rough night. We sat in the breakfast room and attempted to assess the situation. We knew that we had a limited time before the communists came calling. Our first idea was to talk to a friend named Osman who flew as a co-pilot with Bakhtar Airlines, the national airline. The plan was to buy tickets for both families to Herat, a western city bordering Iran. When we were close to landing, we would pretend that we were being highjacked to Meshed, a border city inside Iran. We would seek asylum from the Iranian government, which we would have been granted without any difficulty, as we were members of the Afghan ruling family. This was a sound plan, so we thought, except that our friend refused to go along with it. We continued to brainstorm over the next couple of days, but the next morning Abdullah did not come as usual. Since the phones were disconnected, I could not call him. With no word of him by the next day, I sent Jan Ali to his house to see what was wrong. He came back with the startling news that Abdullah, Mahbooba, and their family had been arrested the night before and taken to the infamous Puli Charkhi prison.

The next day my mother, being very concerned about our well-being, returned from Europe with my sister. In the afternoon of the third day of the communist takeover, I was at my parent's house when Mr. Noor Ahmad Etemadi, Tamim's father, who had just come to Kabul a few days ago for an official meeting with Daoud, came in to see Tamim. As soon as he arrived, the servant came in to say that soldiers had come to the door and were asking for Mr. Etemadi. Without flinching or looking concerned, he pulled his long body out of the chair and followed the servant. We followed him to the outside door. Out on the street were about half a dozen soldiers in battle uniforms standing by their military vehicles with machine guns strapped to their shoulders. They escorted Mr. Etemadi in the second vehicle and left in a hurry.

We were very concerned about his fate. That evening there was a call from Babrak Karmal, the head of the Parcham (Flag) Communist party. He very politely asked me if he could speak to Tamim. I handed the phone to Tamim and we all gathered around him to hear the news.

After hanging up, he told us that Karmal had told him that he had deep respect for his father, that they were treating him as a guest, and were holding him at the Ministry of Foreign Affairs. Since Mr. Etemadi suffered from an acute stomach ailment, he needed his medication. Karmal said that he would send a car for the medicine, which he did, and the medication was sent.

The next we heard about Mr. Etemadi was that he had been moved to Puli Charkhi Prison along with many other political prisoners. Plans were made that Tamim and my sister would deliver food to him every day with a thermos full of tea. It was agreed that so long as the thermos was sent back, he was all right. If the thermos was not returned, it meant that he was killed.

As for the rest of us, we were practically under house arrest. With no telephone and unable to venture out of the house, it almost felt like we were in jail.

On the fourth day of the takeover I was visited by a military officer who was a friend of the family. He told me about what was happening around the country, and all the news was bad. People were being massacred everywhere, including military personnel, former government employees, teachers, religious figures, and business people. He told me that mass graves had been dug within the military compounds at Puli Charkhi and that people were being buried alive (those mass graves still exist today). He said that the communists did not use bullets, but would line up the people along the edge of these graves and then use a club to hit them on the head. They were then pushed into the graves *en masse* and a bulldozer covered them with dirt. Most were not dead when they fell into the pit.

Senior government officials, members of King Zahir Shah's family, military officers, and dignitaries were all taken to the Puli Charkhi Prison. The more I heard, the more I was convinced that it was time to leave Afghanistan. I did not need to think it over any longer when my military contact warned me that I had been placed on a list of ten individuals to be executed. He urged me to leave the country immediately because a man by the name of Taroun, a close compatriot of Hafizullah Amin and a staunch communist, had put my name on the list. My contact did not know why Taroun had targeted me. Maybe he had been denied entry into my restaurant one night and was holding a grudge. He was insane.

For our next plan, which had to be realized soon, we relied on my six-foot bodyguard, Sarwar (whom Sahar called "Star Wars"), who had saved my life on two different occasions and was a very trusted individual. Through him I made arrangements to escape from the country. He was to contact a Pakistani bus driver and offer him money to take me across the border to Pakistan.

Before I could leave I had to make sure that Maribeth and the children were safely out of the country. We made arrangements for Maribeth to meet with the new US Ambassador, Adolph Dubs. Being blonde and blue eyed, she could move around the city quite freely, and that made it possible for me to send information and reports to faithful associates through the Embassy. She would take a taxi to the center of the city, change taxis, and then go to the US Embassy to deliver the information. This was a dangerous act, but Maribeth insisted on doing it. We decided to write a letter on behalf of Mr. Paul Blawie, Maribeth's father, stating that he had been diagnosed with cancer and that he wanted to see his daughter. Beth took this letter to Ambassador Dubs and explained our plans for leaving Afghanistan.

Ambassador Dubs took the letter and went to see Hafizullah Amin, who was then the Minister of Foreign Affairs. At first Amin rejected the request, stating that Maribeth was now an Afghan citizen through marriage. But Dubs insisted and demanded that Beth be issued an exit visa because in the eyes of the US government she was an American citizen. Amin gave in and made orders for the visa to be issued.

I took Maribeth to the Ministry of Foreign affairs the very next day, and her visit was a crisis from the start. To enter the offices of the Ministry of Foreign Affairs, she first had to walk through a metal detector. She placed her handbag and jewelry on the table and walked through the door. The alarm buzzer went off. She searched her entire body, but could not find any metal that would set off the alarm. After many attempts through the door, she realized that the only metal item on her was the metal clasp in her bra. She explained this to the policewoman on duty and was finally allowed to pass through.

At first, Amin gave her the permission to leave, but would not allow the children to go with her. She came out with tears in her eyes to tell me the news, and we went directly to see Ambassador Dubs. When we told him about Amin's decision, he picked up the phone and in a terse voice told Amin that the children must accompany their mother. After a brief exchange of words, he hung up and told us to go back to the Ministry. We did, and this time a letter was waiting for Maribeth with Amin's private secretary, giving permission for her and our daughters to leave Afghanistan.

Having received the exit visas, we began to lay plans for my escape. Sarwar contacted the Pakistani Bus Transport company and told them to make arrangements for my trip to Pakistan. At that time, there was a daily bus service from Kabul to Peshawar, a city about 35 miles beyond the border into Pakistan.

The next task was to get my visas for traveling to Pakistan and the USA. The Pakistani visa was issued in my forged Afghan passport, but the US Embassy Consulate gave me a letter to the US Embassy in Rawalpindi, Pakistan, for the issuance of a visa, as they did not want the communist guards to see a US visa stamped in my passport. If they saw such a document, there was no doubt they would send me to jail. The letter stated that for my security as a member of the former royal family of Afghanistan, they thought it wise to have the visa issued in Pakistan.

All of these arrangements took a couple of months to materialize, and finally, by September of 1978, I was ready to embark on my journey into the unknown. Taroun did not dare touch me so long as Maribeth was in Afghanistan. He was waiting for her to leave before dealing with me. (I later learned that after my departure Taroun was adamant about finding me and almost prevented my brother's wife from leaving. He told her he would not allow her to leave until I showed up, but he finally relented and she was free to go.)

At the last moment before my departure Maribeth decided that instead of flying out of Kabul she was going to accompany me on the bus. Try as I might, I could not change her mind, so I agreed.

All of our plans were made in secret. Only the closest members of the family were aware of our escape. Our servants had been indoctrinated and were reporting all that they heard or saw to the communist secret police, so the night before our departure I told the servants that they had the next day off because I was going to take my wife and the children to the airport. They knew that Beth was allowed to leave, but had no idea of my plans.

Over the months I had let my hair grow long and my beard shaggy in preparation for my escape. Dressed in dirty jeans, a tee shirt, and a leather vest with fringe, I looked every bit like one of the many hippies traveling through Afghanistan. Early the next morning after breakfast we left the house exactly the way it was and took just two suitcases filled with clothes. The night before, while packing, I insisted that Beth take all of her formal evening gowns with her, as we may have to attend official parties on the way to the US. The second suitcase was filled with children's clothes.

The allowable amount of money per traveler was $200, so between us we had a grand total of $400. Luckily, a month before the communist takeover, I had sold a large shipment of polyethylene bags to the Ministry of Agriculture and the South Korean Company Daewoo owed me about $10,000. The money was still with their agents in Karachi, so I asked them to keep the money there until I arrived.

Before our departure, I had given my Jaguar to an acquaintance and sold my beautiful MG TC to a member of the United Nations for a paltry sum of $5,000, which he promised to send to me when I arrived in the States. We left some of our valuables and antiques with my brother who had made plans with an American family to ship them out with their household goods. Abandoning all the businesses that I had established since 1970, I was on my way to an unknown future with a wife and two infants. All I had to do was smuggle myself out of the country disguised as a foreign hippie. What could possibly go wrong?

CHAPTER 10

DEPARTURE FROM KABUL

On the morning of August 28, 1978, we launched Sarwar's risky escape plan by piling into my brother's car and heading for the bus terminal.

When we arrived at the bus station, Sarwar found our bus driver and huddled the three of us together to go over the plan. He explained to me that when we got to the border, the driver would collect all the passengers' passports to get them stamped, according to the border police policy. The driver nodded in agreement. After the driver left the bus to deal with the border officials I was to step out of the bus and mingle with crowds outside. Upon completing the process, the driver would call for the passengers to get on board, and I would follow them and take my seat. It sounded simple enough, but after shaking hands with the driver and watching him head toward the bus I downed a prescription sedative to calm my nerves.

A few minutes later we boarded a bus whose surface was covered with multicolored paintings of lions, birds, and mountain scenery. Beth and the girls occupied the front seats, with Sarwar sitting in the adjoining seat for their protection. I went to the back of the bus and sat next to two long-haired hippies. I blended right in with my long hair and beard, torn and dirty jeans, leather vest, and bandana tied around my head. I looked every bit like any of the thirty or so hippie passengers scattered about the bus.

When the bus started to roll, I introduced myself to my seat companions and told them about my escape plan. They whispered my plan to the other passengers sitting nearby, and soon thereafter, one of the passengers handed me a guitar. I told him that I did not play the guitar, but he said that when they started to play, I should join in as if I did. I would soon learn the wisdom behind their method.

When we reached the beginning of Kabul Gorge, a narrow opening between high craggy mountain ranges through which the Kabul River twisted like a snake after following the entire length of the road, we were stopped by a roadblock manned by several communist soldiers. As soon as the bus stopped, my companions lit up their hashish pipes, began strumming on their guitars, and signaled me to do the same. I hesitated until I saw the soldiers climbing into the bus. They started to check the passports up front. By the time they got to the where we were sitting, the bus was filled with hash smoke and the noise of our guitars and voices singing as loud as our lungs could blow. Fortunately, the smoke hid my nervousness and the sweat pouring down my face, but I wondered if they could hear the pounding of my heart.

The soldiers looked at us with disgust, turned around, and strode off the bus. The guitar ploy had worked. We repeated this routine through the next eight checkpoints and achieved the same results. By the time we got to the Torkham border, I had inhaled enough secondhand smoke to become just as stoned as the rest of my companions.

The Torkham border between Afghanistan and Pakistan is a very historical site. British forces tried to invade Afghanistan at this border three times in the nineteenth century and were defeated and chased back each time. On the Pakistan side of the border lay the famous Khyber Pass. The border area was filled with throngs of people sitting in teahouses and smoking hookahs (water pipes), eating lamb kebobs, or just walking around. I wondered how many of them were like me, waiting for a chance to get to freedom. Oil tankers were lined up in a row waiting their turn to cross the border. I was told that some of the escapees were hiding inside the tankers, crammed into a secret compartment welded in the front section of the empty tank. Regrettably, due to the heat and lack of oxygen, several of these stowaways would perish, as had others who had made the trip. Others,

I later learned, like my cousin Zia and his wife Fourier, crossed the border on the back of a donkey. Compared to those other poor souls, I was in a much better position.

When the bus stopped at the Torkham border, the driver collected all the passports and went to the visa booth. I got off the bus and slowly walked into a crowd, where I waited for the signal to get back on board. I watched the driver return to the bus and whisper something to Sarwar, who was standing by the door. The message must not have been good because Sarwar looked bothered as he made his way toward me.

Standing with his back to me, he whispered that the police had changed the rules and now every passenger had to get his own passport stamped at the counter. While he was relaying this to me, I heard Sahar yell, "Daddy! Daddy!" I looked up to find her sticking her head out of the bus window and waving to me. Without answering her, I quickly moved behind the bus where Sahar could not see me.

I should have panicked, but thanks to the pill and hash smoke I calmly took the passport from Sarwar and waited until half of the passengers had lined up in front of the counter. I then joined the line and, holding my passport in my right hand, opened it to an empty page. By the time I got to the counter the police were automatically stamping the pages without looking up—just as I had hoped. I placed my passport on the table, the officer stamped it, and I picked it up and walked away. Exhaling a sigh of relief, I felt great and could not hold back a smile as I walked back to the bus. My excitement was short lived, however. Sarwar once again stepped over to me and whispered that I now had to take my passport to the border police chief because all Afghans were required to have their passports registered.

When I walked into the border station office I saw a long table at the opposite end of the room. Behind this table sat a police captain with his tell-tale moustache (all communist members wore moustaches, but no beards) and a cigarette dangling from the corner of his mouth. Two lower-ranked officers sat on either side of him. As I walked toward the table, I noticed a big open book in front of the police chief. I glanced at the book as I handed him my passport and my heart took a jolt— one of the two names on the pages was Beth's. Even though the name in my passport was Abdul Ali without the Seraj, it would not take a rocket scientist to connect Maribeth Seraj with Abdul Ali Seraj. Since

I was told that I could not leave Afghanistan with my wife and kids, any fool could have made the connection between us by connecting the two names.

As I pondered my dire situation and wondered how long I had before I was arrested, I heard the door behind me open and a voice tell the captain that he was needed outside for some emergency. Still holding my passport, the captain asked one of his lieutenants to see what was going on. The man at the door insisted that the captain attend to the problem, so without looking at my passport, the captain dropped it in front of the officer next to him and reluctantly got up and walked out. The junior officer entered my passport number and wished me a safe journey. Once outside I ran past Sarwar, who was staying behind to return to Kabul, and hurriedly went to the bus. Before I could get in, I heard Sahar again call out, "Daddy! Daddy!" Hoping that no one outside heard her, I got in the bus and walked passed Maribeth and my daughters, ignoring Sahar's outstretched arms. I reached my seat and sat down with a deep sigh of relief.

Grabbing the guitar firmly to my chest, I waited for the driver to start the bus.

///////////

The Torkham border was the gateway to Pakistan. A huge chain stretched across the highway on the Afghan side, beyond which lie about 100 meters of barren turf called the "No Man's Land." On the other side another chain bisected the road on the Pakistan side of the border. Freedom was a mere 200 meters away.

As the bus rolled slowly towards the chain on the Afghan side, the same mustached communist captain ran to the bus, signaled the driver to stop, and climbed aboard. My first thought was that he had heard my daughter. Surrounded by my fellow rag-tag hippies, I held my breath and waited.

The officer immediately began checking the passports. He started with Beth. After viewing her passport, he continued down the aisle, checking each passenger's documents. I was paralyzed in my seat, waiting for him to discover me and pull me off the bus. I looked at the back of Maribeth's head and thought that it may be the last time I ever see her or our two girls. What if the officer had discovered they were my family and was ready to haul us all off to prison? My mind raced with images of prison, torture, and execution. I was ready to die, but I could not endure the thought of my family suffering for my sake. Why did I let Maribeth return when my country was in such turmoil? Just as the captain got to about two rows in front of me, the same soldier who had burst into his office a few minutes ago once again call out to him to tell him that there was an important phone call from Kabul.

The officer looked around the bus, past my half-hidden face behind the guitar, and reluctantly got off the bus.

As soon as he was gone the driver gunned the motor and the bus lurched across the first set of lowered chains. I closed my eyes and waited until I felt the bus tires cross the second set of chains. Freedom! I opened my eyes to see Beth running down the aisle towards me. I jumped out of my seat and grabbed her, and as we stood in the aisle in a long embrace everyone broke into applause and shouting.

Free at last!

Since no one had eaten anything since we left Kabul, we asked the driver to stop at the first *chai khana* tea house he came across. A few minutes later we all lumbered out of the bus and took our seats in a small, shabby tea house. It could have been falling down around us and still been the most beautiful place I had ever seen. I felt a pang of hunger and immediately ordered fried eggs. Maribeth sat next to me, cuddling little Safia in her arms. Sahar sat on my lap, sucking her pinkie as was her habit.

When the eggs finally arrived, I noticed that they were covered with a moving black blanket. As the waiter put the plate in front of me, what appeared as a black cloth was nothing more than flies covering the eggs. The flies did not deter me from digging into the food. The delicious taste of those eggs followed by local bread, *chapatti*, and tea still lingers in my mouth. Nothing beats the taste of freedom.

After breakfast and an uneventful trip through border passport control, we made our way to Peshawar.

Winding our way through the Khyber Pass and its surrounding Spin Ghar mountain range, I recalled that this region had once been Afghan territory. After the defeat of the British at the second Anglo/Afghan war (the Battle of Maiwand in 1878), Mortimer Durrand, the commander in charge of the British forces, drew a line on the map and declared it a line of defense between the British and Afghan forces.

My great grandfather King Amir Abdurrahman was forced to sign that treaty to prevent further war with the British. The commander's stroke on the map became known as the Durand Line. When Pakistan was separated from India in 1946, this part of our country became part of Pakistan.

/////////////

The bus rambled on for another eleven hours before finally arriving in Peshawar. The ancient, garbage-strewn city streets were filled with masses of people. All types of vehicles, from camel-drawn carts and motorcycle taxis to bright multicolored trucks and water buffalos tried to squeeze themselves though the crowds. Eager to get to the Dean's Hotel, which had been recommended to us by the Pakistan Embassy, we packed ourselves into a horse-drawn buggy, the only mode of transport we could find. We sat back-to-back in the opposite-facing seats—me in the front and Maribeth and the girls in the back—with our suitcases wedged in the front. The driver got in the front seat with me, and with the snap of a long whip the horse jolted and began to move.

After a short trip the buggy stopped in front of the old hotel, a landmark of the colonial era built in 1913 and famous for its former guests such as Rudyard Kipling and Winston Churchill. I paid the buggy driver $2 in Pakistani rupees and carried our bags into the lobby. After checking in, we were led to our room by a turbaned hotel employee. The room was quite large, with two double beds and a ceiling fan. The bathroom was also spacious, clean, and modern.

After a very restful night, the next morning I contacted the Daewoo representative and asked him to make arrangements to send my money to Islamabad. Then we checked out of the hotel and boarded another horse-drawn buggy to set off for Cantonment Station and the next leg of our journey. I purchased first-class train tickets for the 90-mile journey to Islamabad and then followed the signs to the tracks, where we waited for the signal to board. Even though we had purchased the best tickets, the accommodations on the rickety old train were anything but first rate. The cabin consisted of two, long, bench-like seats with two bunks, one above the other. The door to the cabin could not close and the windows were jammed open. The floor was absolutely filthy.

Since the ride would be only a couple of hours long, we did not mind the condition of our "first-class" cabin. As the steam locomotive chugged along, we enjoyed the scenery and villages through which we passed. We watched women working in the fields, water buffalo foraging along the streams, and children running and waving to the train.

About an hour into our journey, the train came to an abrupt halt. I peered out of the window and saw passengers climbing down from the train onto the tracks and yelling, "Engine glia! Engine ghia!" Having a good knowledge of Urdu, the language spoken in Pakistan, I realized that they were shouting that the engine was gone. I looked up the tracks and saw the locomotive rushing away from the rest of the train at a high speed.

Our fellow passengers informed us that the coupling to the locomotive had broken off and that the train engineer was unaware that he had left the rest of the train behind. After about a half hour, we heard the locomotive's whistle and saw the engine returning to the train. With a silly grin on his face, the engineer backed the engine and reconnected it to the rest of the train.

"Hooray!" Maribeth said to the girls. "We're off again!" This time we made it to Islamabad without further incidents. I hired two "red caps" to carry our two suitcases and rented a taxi to take us to the Dean's Hotel in Islamabad. I was certain that the hotel in the capitol city would be at least as comfortable as the Dean's in Peshawar, and looked forward to settling everyone in for another delightfully restful night.

After checking in we were led to a spacious room near the swimming pool. We immediately changed into our bathing suits and jumped into the pool. Maribeth held Safia while I set Sahar on my shoulders, giving her a piggy back ride. She was screaming with delight and it felt great to finally give the children a taste of normal family life.

Early the next morning we went to the US Embassy and submitted my letter to the consulate section. They were very gracious and within the hour issued me an immigrant visa with all the necessary documents.

After returning to the hotel, Maribeth called her family in the US to let them know that we were safe and sound. Mr. Blawie told her that he was going to wire plane tickets to her and the children. I would purchase mine on my own.

I called Daewoo to arrange the money transfer and was told that Pakistani law forbid sending dollars, so they would have to send me Pakistani rupees. Not to worry though, they said, because I could exchange the rupees for dollars at the Pakistan National Bank. When the money arrived, I purchased my airline ticket in rupees and decided to go to the National Bank the next day. It so happened, however, that the three days were national holidays and the banks were going to be closed.

Since our flight was in two days, we were left in a dilemma. We had over six hundred thousand rupees that we could not take out of the country because of currency regulations. While we were pondering our situation, the waiter brought us our evening tea. I gave him a huge tip of more than four times the cost of our food. Since we had money to burn, I decided to spend as much of it as I could over the next two days. Soon rumor got around the hotel about this big tipper. Thereafter, every time I rang for a waiter, several would respond and they could not do enough to please us. Beth suggested that maybe we should go to the US Embassy and see if they could help us convert our rupees. That was a great idea. One of the marine guards bought our rupees and gave us a check on a US bank.

The next evening, we boarded a TWA flight to London, and after the long trip the airline booked us a room in a downtown London hotel. Our flight to the US was scheduled for the next day. We boarded a bus at the airport, and when we arrived at our hotel, Sahar got car sick and threw up as we were getting off the bus. I picked her up and carried her and one of the suitcases into the hotel. Beth followed with Safia and the other suitcase full of evening gowns that she had not used since we left Afghanistan.

The elevator was so small that it could only carry one person with one suitcase at a time. Beth and Safia went up first and then I followed with Sahar. We had a good night's sleep, and the next morning we piled up in a double-decker bus and headed to the Heathrow airport. After checking in, we decided to have an English breakfast before going to our gate. Everything had gone smoothly since our escape over the Afghanistan border, so we were more relaxed than we had been for weeks. I smiled at Maribeth and held Sahar's hand as we rode the escalator to the dining area on the upper floor. All of a sudden Sahar let go of my hand, and before I could grab her she tripped and fell backward down the escalator. I tried to catch her, but I also tripped and we both went tumbling down the moving steps. Fortunately, a passenger had seen our plight and pushed the stop button. I rushed over to pick up Sahar, who was terrified and crying, but unhurt, thank God. I, however, had a broken pinky. We decided against breakfast and went to the boarding area. Two hours later we were in the air and on our way to New York.

///////////

Flying across the Atlantic Ocean, with Maribeth and the children safely seated next to me, I started to feel an emptiness that had been a long time in coming. The events, anxieties, and planning that had preoccupied me over the past few months had not allowed me to think about what I had lost. Now I had time to reminisce about my life, my extended family, my country, and the uncertain future.

I began to reflect on my royal history, an aristocratic life of comfort and leisure, the land of my forefathers, my many business ventures, and most important, my identity.

In Afghanistan, my family's very name drew respect. Regardless of where we went, doors were open to us. We lived the life of the silver spoon. Even though times had changed from the time my father was a child growing up in the palace, we were still Afghanistan. We were the land, and the people paid absolute allegiance to us. Not out of fear, but out of respect for our family history and tribal blood connections.

We lived a life common among most members of royal families. Although our palaces lay in ruins after the 1929 revolution and being carried on sedan chairs was a thing of the past, as children we each had a maid assigned to us. We had private tutors. Most of us attended the same French Academy in Kabul, the Lycée Isteqlal. All classes were divided alphabetically, with Class Alef (A) the top grade and reserved for the princes. We were all enrolled in this grade.

We all went to the military officers' school and graduated as first lieutenants. Most of us were sent overseas to finish our higher education abroad. Each family member's choice of college was based on what foreign language he had studied in school. Those with English language background were sent to either England or the United States. Since I had begun to speak English when my father was assigned to the Afghan embassy in Pakistan, and I was not in favor of England because of our volatile history with the British, I opted for the US. My family decided that I should attend the University of Connecticut, where I graduated with a degree in Agricultural Economics and Business/Public Management.

Upon returning from college, a good number of royal family members were sent to work in the Ministry of Foreign Affairs, but I knew that was not the life for me. I built a discotheque instead, and redefined Kabul as the gathering place of prominent visitors, globetrotting explorers—and spies. My business and social ventures that followed not only provided a life of purpose, but also instilled in me an even greater sense of responsibility toward the people of my country.

As the lights came up in the airplane and the aroma of coffee began to wake up the passengers, I wondered when I would be able to return to my homeland. Would a communist regime wipe out centuries of culture and history and destroy Afghanistan as we all knew it? This question lay heavy in my heart, but it was also time to look ahead. As the plane taxied to the gate at John F. Kennedy International Airport, I hugged Maribeth and the girls and felt grateful for everyone who had helped us arrive safely in our new home.

CHAPTER 11

A NEW BEGINNING

While standing in the passport control line at Kennedy Airport with Beth and the children, I heard an announcement calling for a Mr. "Seragh" to come to the information desk. I thought it was interesting that the name was similar to mine, but then forgot about it. After passport control, we were guided to a special area for those with immigrant visas where they took my passport and papers for processing. They said that it would take a while, as there were others ahead of me. Exhausted, we sat on the bench across from this room and leaned on each other. Little Safia was asleep in her mother's arms and Sahar sat next to me, hugging my arm tightly and sucking her index finger.

Watching the throngs of people in the hall, I noticed a well-dressed couple walking and pointing towards us. When they got to where we were sitting, the woman asked me if I was Mr. Seragh from Afghanistan. I told her that my name was Seraj. She apologized and then, after greeting Maribeth, asked us to come with them. The man told us that they were with the US government and had been sent to welcome us to the United States. When I told them that the immigration office had my passport, the man immediately went to the office. Within minutes he was back with my passport and papers.

133

After welcoming us, the woman left, but the man stayed behind to help us with our luggage. While carrying Sahar in his arms, he led us to the customs area and asked me to identify our suitcases. When I did, he pulled out our luggage and after showing his ID to the customs agents led us to the exit, where Mr. and Mrs. Blawie and Sharon, Beth's youngest sister, were waiting for us. I thanked the gentleman for all he had done, said goodbye, and joined the Blawies.

After many tears of joy and greetings, we all piled into the Blawie's station wagon and headed for Milford, Connecticut, where the Blawies owned a beautiful home right on the beach on Long Island Sound.

//////////

SEPTEMBER 1978, MILFORD, CONNECTICUT

The first evening at the Blawie household at Laurel Beach, a private beach community in Milford, Mr. Blawie asked me to go for a walk with him on the sea wall which ran along the front of all the beach houses. While we were walking, he asked me if I had managed to get any money out. I told him about the limited funds that we had with us and he became very concerned about how we were going to manage. I told him not to worry, as I had a great deal of business experience and did not expect to have any problem landing a good job.

Over the next few days I typed up my resume and called a headhunter office. I went to see the firm's director, a man I will call Mr. Cohn. I handed him my résumé and watched him read it as he sat behind his desk. He shook his head as he turned the pages, and then waved them in the air. He told me in a sarcastic tone of voice that if I thought I could get a job in the US with a name like "Ab-dool All-eye Ser-age I had another thing coming. He suggested that I change my name to Jack or Joe.

I was not only insulted, but dumbfounded at his suggestion. I grabbed my résumé from his hand, ripped it to pieces, threw it to the floor, and told him that there was a thousand-year history behind my name and no money on earth could make me change it. I strode out of his office and didn't look back.

I decided then and there that I was going to work on my own after gaining some experience doing business the American way.

Looking for advice for my job search, I contacted my cousin Waheedullah Tarzi, who was the head of Human Resources at the United Nations in New York. He was my mother's nephew, and his wife, Ayetan, was Mahmood beg Tarzi's granddaughter.

Waheedullah told me that there was an opening in Namibia for a position in overseeing the elections there. The drawback was that due to the security situation, my wife and children could not accompany me. The contract would be for one year. As tempting as the offer was, I did not accept it. I could not be separated from my family for such a long period of time after just having escaped from hell together. They needed me and I, them.

He next suggested that I meet with a Turkish friend of his, Attila Turkan, who owned an export business in New York. I accepted this offer and took the train down to the city to see Attila. His office was located directly across the street from Grand Central Station and had a great view of the Chrysler Building.

I found Attila to be a gentle but shrewd businessman. He was involved in exporting anything that the Middle East wanted from the United States. He welcomed me as a brother and told me point blank that, while he could use my services to create additional markets in the Arab world, he could not offer me a regular salary. With interest rates in the US around 16 percent, money was difficult to come by and business was not so good.

I wanted to use his operation as a learning opportunity, so I accepted his terms of working largely on commission, provided that he covered my traveling cost between Connecticut and New York. He agreed and I started right away.

Since I was responsible for setting up housing for the rest of my family when they arrived from Afghanistan, I rented a house on the beach just two doors down from the Blawies. The huge, three-story home had six bedrooms, six bathrooms, came fully furnished, and included a large yard where the children could play.

As soon as we moved in I decided to put an ad in the local paper seeking warm clothing for the multitude of refugees who were now fleeing Afghanistan and settling in the bare mountains inside Pakistan. Winter was coming and they had nothing more than the clothes on their backs. People responded immediately and started bringing bags of clothes, coats, jackets, shoes, and every other article of clothing imaginable to our house. The charitable attitude of the residents of Milford was overwhelming. In a matter of days, our giant two-car garage was filled to the brim.

A box company donated a large supply of oversized cartons for shipping the clothing, and we spent days wrapping and packing up the clothes. The boxes overflowed onto the parking area of the house and the clothes kept coming. I was about to put in another ad to thank the donors and ask them to hold off on donations until further notice when I was contacted by an Afghan man named Habib Mayar. He told me that he had heard through my cousin about my clothing drive, and since he owned a trucking company he would like to pick up the materials for shipment to the refugees. The best way to get the articles to them was through the Pakistani airline PIA, which had already offered its unused cargo space for us.

Our charitable work received a great deal publicity, including an article in the *Bridgeport Post* by reporter Richard Marrash which brought so much attention that thereafter I was continually invited as a guest speaker to various clubs, universities, and civil and military professional organizations.

The refugee aid program and speaking events took place during the winter of 1978 and spring of 1979. Among the donors was a man by the name of Victor Levinson who owned a meat market and was a good friend of Mrs. Blawie. He had heard that I owned restaurants in Afghanistan and offered me a partnership in setting up a fish market in one of his empty stores in downtown Milford. As we toured the facility, he showed me the built-in cold room that would be perfect for storing fresh fish. Shortly after that the Fisherman's Wharf of Milford was born.

I designed the restaurant along the style of an Afghan fish shop—without the rodents or dirt floors. Customers would choose their fish, order them fried up in the deep fryers I had installed in the kitchen, and enjoy fresh, delicious meals with a hint of Afghan spices. Fisherman's Wharf became quite a successful venture. I enjoyed bringing a touch of my culture to that small corner of the East Coast, but I needed more time to work for my country and people. I decided to sell my share to my partner, Victor, who had made it all happen, and continued with my charitable work for Afghanistan.

As I hung up my apron for the last time, I wondered how my old friends in the fish shops in Kabul were doing.

CHAPTER 12

THE FIGHT AGAINST AFGHAN COMMUNISM AND THE SOVIET INVASION

In the spring of 1979, my cousin Wahid Tarzi suggested that I should contact another cousin, Dr. Bashir Zikria, who was a heart specialist at the Columbia Medical Center in New York City and an avid Afghan supporter. Since he, too, was involved in helping the Afghan people, Wahid thought that it would be a good idea for us to join forces.

In my first meeting with Dr. Zikria we agreed that our first plan of action should be to meet with US Senator Frank Church, Chairman of the Senate Committee on Foreign Relations. I called his office and made an appointment for the last week of August 1979. Three of us arranged to see him: Dr. Zikria; Mr. Rahim, a former member of the Afghan Foreign Ministry; and I. When we got there, we were received by a tall woman who ushered us into the senator's office where she had placed three chairs in a row, like a schoolroom. She set herself on the corner of the senator's desk, and folding her arms across her broad chest, asked us what we wanted from the senator, as he was away for a meeting.

Since I was the chosen spokesperson, I cleared my throat and said that we had come to apprise Senator Church about the situation in Afghanistan. I explained that should the US take its eyes off our country, the effect would be very negative in Iran and the US would lose Iran.

She looked at me with stern eyes and without unfolding her arms waved her index finger in a "no" fashion, and then went on to say that that was not the reason why we were there. She said, in a cold voice, that our reason for coming was because of the fact that as we three were members of the former royal family we expected the US government to help us regain our throne. She continued with her sarcastic remarks stating that the US was in full control of Iran and that nothing was going to happen there. However, she continued, the Carter administration was very concerned about the Pan-Islamic awakening that was taking place from Saudi Arabia to Indonesia.

We were dumbfounded at her attitude and statements. I looked at her and in a sarcastic tone equal to hers asked if she believed that morning 1.2 billion people suddenly woke up around the world and realized that they were Muslims. I told her that in case she was not aware, we have been Muslims, are Muslims, and will be Muslims—all 1.2 billion of us—and the administration should be more concerned about Iran, for surely, they will lose control over that country in a very short time. We got up, and without goodbye niceties, left the senator's office. (I have often wondered what that lady thought when, five months later, the Shah fled Iran and the country transformed into an Islamic Republic headed by Ayatollah Khomeini.)

We did not allow that woman's attitude discourage us. Both Dr. Zikria and I continued our relentless work to help Afghanistan.

In the meantime, President Brezhnev of the Soviet Union was getting very impatient with Amin's bloody policies in Afghanistan. At a meeting in Moscow, President Taraki was instructed to get rid of Amin. Upon his return from Moscow, Taraki attempted to follow his boss's instructions, but before he could carry out the Soviet orders, Amin had Taraki killed and took his place as the President of Afghanistan. (Journalist Rhea Talley Stewart, author of *Fire in Afghanistan*, wrote an article after meeting with Amin in 1979 in which she stated that she felt that since Amin had lost the support of Brezhnev, he was looking for support from the U).

The Red Army, having lost their key communist supporter at the hands of Amin, invaded Afghanistan on December 26, 1979. The Soviet Special Forces killed Amin while he was entertaining his mistress one evening on the terrace of one of our palaces, Tapay Tajbeg. They replaced him with Babrak Karmal, the leader of the Parcham ("flag") communist party, who was at that time living in exile in Moscow.

We expected a very stern response from the United States government, but unfortunately, once again our hopes were dashed. President Carter's only response to this blatant Soviet act was to cancel the US Olympic team's participation in the 1980 Moscow Olympics.

CHAPTER 13

THE REAGAN ERA

When Ronald Reagan won the Republican nomination for the presidency in July 1980, I sent him a telegram on behalf of the Afghan-Americans, congratulating him on his win, and wishing him success in the upcoming elections. Referring to him as "President to be," I beseeched him to help Afghanistan when he took office.

His response to me was very heartwarming. He personally wrote me a letter, thanking me for my kind words and saying that those words meant a great deal to him. He also welcomed my partnership in the cause.

In January 1981, about three weeks after Reagan's inauguration, I received a call from a man who asked to meet with me. At that time, my cousin Timur Shah Hamid, who had formerly worked in the Pan Am airlines office in Kabul, was at our house. I asked the caller why he wanted to meet, and he told me that his government, the US administration, had authorized him to do so. I covered the mouthpiece and relayed his request to Timur and Beth, both of whom were standing next to me. Timur, always the cautious one, warned me that I should not meet with him as he might be a KGB agent sent out to assassinate me, as I was speaking out against the Red Army and the Soviet Union's involvement in Afghanistan. Timur suggested that if I wanted to meet with the man I should not bring him to the house, but choose a public place instead. I agreed.

I told the caller that I would meet him at the McDonald's parking lot off of Exit 34 of I-95, in Milford, CT, at 2:00 p.m. the following day. He agreed. When I tried to describe what I looked like, he told me that he already knew and that he would be driving a red Toyota. After I hung up and told Timur about the color of the car, he gasped and said that he was sure that the caller was a KGB agent. Both Beth and I laughed at his reaction.

The next day, Timur and I put on our London Fog overcoats, looking very much like spies from the movies, and drove to the McDonald's. We got there a good fifteen minutes early and parked my car in a corner from where we could see the interstate ramp. The red car appeared at exactly two o'clock. When he parked, we got out of my car and walked up to him. As planned, I walked to the driver's side and Timur to the passenger side, thus preventing the man from getting out. The caller rolled down his window and greeted me as "Your Highness." I asked for an ID. When he produced one, I noticed that he worked for an intelligence agency. His name was Haldane.

When we were convinced that he was not a KGB agent, I invited him to our house. He followed us in his car, and when we arrived Beth greeted us at the door and, like a good Afghan wife, offered him tea. When she went to the kitchen to make tea, I followed her and, when out of earshot of Mr. Haldane, told her that after serving tea she should stand by the door facing her parent's house. In case of a problem, she should dash over and warn her parents.

After tea was served and Beth disappeared to her post, Haldane introduced himself as an agent of the US government agency noted on his ID and said that he was instructed to talk to me about the type of American weapons that the US could send the newly formed freedom fighters inside Afghanistan and what other type of assistance the US could offer.

I told him that American-made weapons would not be of any use as our people were unfamiliar with them. They were trained on Russian equipment. He said that the US did not possess Russian weaponry. I reminded him that Egyptian President Anwar Sadat possessed a great deal of Russian equipment, and since the US had agreed to send Sadat over $5 billion worth of American weapons, perhaps Sadat could be coaxed into sending some of his Soviet-made weapons to the freedom fighters.

I also requested that since this type of warfare was new to our people, perhaps some of our commanders could be sent to Egypt to be trained by US military experts. I then named a long list of additional materials that would be critical to the freedom fighter's effort. The agent wrote down everything that I requested. He folded the list, put it in his pocket, and got up to leave. He told us that he was merely a messenger, but he would make sure that the list got into the right hands.

Three weeks later, I got another call from Haldane, requesting another meeting. This time he came directly to our house. Once inside, he produced a list of his own which contained about 120 names of Afghan communist members, starting with Babrak Karmal, the new Soviet-selected President of the Democratic Republic of Afghanistan. He told me that his agency wanted to know who they were.

/////////

I took the list from him and told him to come back in one week. During that week I shared the list with my father and one cousin, Zaid Siddiq, who was very familiar with these people. Working together, we identified each and every one on the list and gave the information to Haldane when he came back. On that trip, he told me that my list of requests was in the right hands. I later learned that out of everything I had wished for, two important requests were granted: Soviet weaponry from Egypt and the training of some of our commanders by the US military in Egypt.

After that, I never heard from Mr. Haldane again. But about three months later I got a phone call from a different, huskier voice. Without introducing himself, he too asked to meet with me, but not in my house. He was more of the cloak-and-dagger type, suggesting a meeting at the Sykorsky Airport in Bridgeport, Connecticut. He directed me to sit at the coffee shop counter in the airport hallway, where he would join me. He, too, told me that he knew who I was.

His suggestion of sitting at the counter, with my back to the people, made me a bit uneasy. I discussed the matter with a fellow Afghan, Hamidullah Makhmoor, who had graduated from a US military college and was also living in Milford. I asked him to accompany me and sit across from me. In case of danger, he was to warn me so I could move out of the way of a thrusting knife or any other weapon. I figured that if the intent was to assassinate me, a knife would be silent and therefore the most likely weapon.

Hamidullah and I went to the airport and seated ourselves in our respective places. Soon after I sat down, I felt a tap on my shoulder. I turned around to find a huge, handlebar-mustached individual standing behind me. Without a greeting or cordiality, he asked me to follow him to the meeting room upstairs. I told him that I had a friend with me and that he must accompany us. He agreed, so I waved to Hamidullah to come with us. We walked up a long flight of stairs to a conference room with a long table.

The three of us sat down at the head of the table. As soon as we were seated, the gargantuan man looked at me and said that he wanted me to introduce an Afghan to him who could go to the Afghan/Pakistan border and make a survey of what was going on and what was needed among the seven camps that were set up to receive the refugees and the freedom fighters. But no at time anyone should get the wind that the person was working for the agency.

I volunteered to go. He did not accept my offer, saying that as a member of the former ruling family I would easily be recognized, which would endanger my life. I looked at Hamidullah and said, "How about him?"

Handlebar moustache man accepted my suggestion to send Hamidullah on the mission. After that, he gave Hamidullah a telephone number for the person who would make arrangements for his trip. He then left, waving goodbye. I never got his name. After that meeting, I did not see or hear from the handlebar or Hamidullah until years later when I ran into Hamidullah in Kabul after my return to my homeland.

///////////

One by one, immediate members of my family arrived in Milford. First, it was my brother's wife Karen with their daughter Tammy. She stayed for a few days and then left to be with her parents in Utah. Then my brother arrived, only to leave a few days later to join his family. He was followed by my parents, my sister, and Tamim, her husband. I was very proud that I had rented a house large enough to accommodate them all, but it was not to be. My sister got a job in New York, so she and Tamim moved there. My parents wanted to be among the large group of relatives who had settled in Flushing, New York, so they moved there. I was left with a huge house that was much too big for our family's needs, so we decided to cut costs and move to an apartment near the beach in Milford.

Because my funds were running low, I needed to get gainfully employed. The only opportunity available that would give me an income and also the free time to continue to work for Afghanistan was in real estate. After attending classes, I earned my license and went into commercial sales. Most of my clients in the region were Japanese. Just as I had hoped, real estate gave me a good income and the flexible schedule I needed.

In 1983, I became the proud father of another beautiful daughter, whom we named Alia. Even though all three of our daughters were born in the United States, Alia was the only one who did not see Afghanistan as a child. Our apartment had only two bedrooms, so the girls had to share one room. The older girls, being close in age, were bonded, so that left me to be a playmate for Alia. I did not mind the job one bit. In fact, I found it very enjoyable. I loved all three daughters equally.

The apartment was very small for a family of five, so in 1985, after selling a major piece of property, I earned enough in commissions to buy a house in Milford. It was situated on a cul-de-sac and the neighbors were families with children like us. Life was good.

With mortgage payments due every month, I decided to look elsewhere for an opportunity to make a steady income. I contacted my cousin Dr. Mohd Afzal Aslami, who lived in Sturbridge, Massachusetts. Doctor Aslami, whom I called Afzal, was the co-inventor of fiber optics and had recently purchased an electro-magnetic relay company called Allied Controls based in Waterbury, Connecticut. He offered me the position of vice president of sales and marketing, and I immediately accepted. I began selling relays to the US military, telephone companies, and customers overseas.

No sooner had I started work for Afzal's company when, in mid-1986, Mrs. Blawie was diagnosed with breast cancer. This was devastating news for the whole family. Mrs. Blawie was the center of the entire family, a rose around whom the butterflies fluttered. The news of her having incurable cancer had a great effect on all of us.

Mrs. Blawie underwent surgery, and after she recovered, Mr. Blawie, in honor of his wife's sixty-second birthday, invited the whole family—nine daughters, their spouses, and his three sons—on a cruise to Bermuda and the Bahamas. It was a most memorable journey. I had never been on a cruise and needless to say, I started suffering from seasickness. But Maribeth had planned ahead and brought ear patches for just such an occasion. After placing a medicated patch behind my ear, I was fine.

When we landed in the Bahamas, everyone decided to go shopping in the straw market. At a hat shop, my brothers-in-law wanted to buy hats, but the storekeeper was asking more than $30 for the hats. I felt that that was too much, so I offered to negotiate the man down. Coming from the East, I had mastered the art of bargaining, and they were happy to let me have a go at it. I brought the price down to $20 and we all agreed that that was a fair price. They cheerfully paid the price and proudly wore their straw hats for the rest of the voyage.

Once back home in Milford, I went to a department store to buy some gifts for the kids who had been left behind with my parents. While at the store, I noticed the same straw hats on a rack. My curiosity compelled me to check out the price tags, and I discovered that they were selling for $10 each. I was so embarrassed that I kept the secret for many years before telling my in-laws.

In the summer of 1987 Mrs. Blawie's health took a turn for the worse. Upon examination, she was told that the cancer had spread to other vital organs in her body, and she was given a very short time for survival.

The news drained the energy out of all her children, but the effect was far greater on Maribeth. She felt that she was perhaps being punished for not adhering to her parents' Catholic religion during her hippie years. Both of her parents were very involved with the Church; in fact, when I first visited the Blawie household in 1969, I saw a small chapel on their estate. Later in life, Mr. Blawie had been ordained as a deacon and Mrs. Blawie was also very involved in the affairs of the Church. No one was ready for her to pass away at such a young age of 62. After the latest diagnosis, she became bedridden.

When the time came, the whole family was around her. I went to her bedside, and holding her hand said a silent prayer for her. She squeezed my hand and then let go. Not long after that she breathed her last breath and silently departed from this earth.

I could not take the grief in the room, so I stepped outside for a cigarette. My brother-in-law Arthur Woodstone joined me and we both grieved in silence for having lost a great friend. That is what she was to us, a friend.

After the death of Mrs. Blawie I noticed a great change in Maribeth. She started attending church every Sunday and got involved in church affairs and religious functions. In short, she made a 360-degree turn towards the Catholic religion, which she had avoided for so long. She submerged herself as if to make up for all the years of staying away. Even though all of this was new to me, I could not argue with her decision. I had never been a strict religious person, but I could not deny her the experience of discovering her religion. Instead, I got totally engrossed with my new work at Allied Controls and started to travel to different parts of the country to meet with clients.

My work trips put me in contact with different types of people from all walks of life. Among those I met was a former senator from Pennsylvania, Don Ritter, a Republican. He had been a friend of Afghanistan from the outset of the Soviet invasion, and had established the Afghanistan-America Foundation based in Washington, DC. With my family safely secured in our own home and with a steady income, I dedicated more time to Afghanistan's affairs, this time with the additional help from Senator Ritter. He generously set up meetings for me with congressmen and State Department officials, opening new doors that I hoped would lead to new positive results in Afghanistan.

CHAPTER 14

THE RUSSO-AFGHAN WAR AND THE RE-EMERGENCE OF THE TALIBAN/AL QAEDA

President Reagan kept his word and gave Afghanistan all the assistance it needed in its war against the Red Army. The longer the war lasted, the deeper I got involved in the affairs of the country.

My theme was the same wherever and whenever I was invited to speak about the war: help the Afghans win the war. The Soviet atrocities being committed against the Afghan people were no less tragic than those of the Holocaust. Millions of our people became refugees. Four million fled to the mountains of Pakistan, two million fled to Iran and close to one million were spread around the globe, from Australia to Europe to the United States. One-and-a-half million were killed inside the country and another one-half million died through migratory genocide.

The killing machine of the Red Army was the Mi-17 and Mi-24 Hind helicopters. These armor-plated machines were invincible against bullets, and one helicopter would devastate an entire village in a matter of minutes. Our ill-armed people fought bravely against the enemy. In the beginning, before arms arrived from Egypt and elsewhere, the tribal fighters used anything that they came across against the Red soldiers. There were cases in which a freedom fighter would soak blankets with kerosene, jump on a Russian tank, wrap it around the turret, and then set it afire. The heat would force the occupants to open the hatch. Once the hatch was opened, our fighters would shoot the enemy. In other cases, our fighters would wrap dynamite around their bodies and throw themselves under the tank to blow it up. They even found a way to down the Hind assault helicopters. The fighters would send word to the Russian camp that a group of freedom fighters were gathering in a valley. Then they would send sharpshooters up the mountain on either side of the valley. When the helicopter approached, the group would gather below, and the snipers would shoot the pilot in his seat. Fortunately, only the belly of the Hind was armor plated, not the windshield or cockpit windows.

The Red Army paid us back by gathering groups of citizens, throwing them into a room, pouring gasoline in the room, and setting it on fire. They also rounded up groups of Afghans and ran them over with their tanks.

In the farmlands, the fields were irrigated by a system of aqueducts. When the Russians would approach a village, the inhabitants would hide in these ducts. The Red Army soldiers would bring their fuel tankers and pour gasoline into the ducts, set it on fire, and burn all the men, women, and children alive.

In the cities, the vegetable sellers got their own revenge against the enemy. After closing shop, which was nothing more than pulling a sheet over the merchandise, they knew that the Soviet soldiers would steal their vegetables. The shopkeepers would put rat poison on the items closest to the street. In the morning, poisoned enemy soldiers would be found lying dead on the street.

In that war, the freedom fighters fought like brave soldiers. There were no suicide bombers.

I happened to play an indirect role in bringing the bloody war to an end, and in the process brought the Soviet empire to its knees with the help of the United States. It all started with a speech I gave to 500 US Naval Academy pilots at the Naval Submarine Base in Groton, Connecticut, where I told my very attentive audience about the war and the destruction that the armor-plated Hind helicopters were inflicting across the country and how the Russian MiGs flew around unchallenged, dropping their deadly arsenal wherever.

After my presentation and the usual photo-taking opportunities with a prince of Afghanistan, I was taken aside by two officers, whose names shall remain unknown, and given two transparencies showing where the Red Army had used chemical weapons against my people. The documents even detailed what type of chemical weapons were used on what part of the country. In addition, they told me that I should ask US officials for Stinger missiles because, as they explained, the Stinger was the only weapon capable of bringing down Hind helicopters and MiGs.

I was very excited to hear about this weapon. With its infrared technology, the Stinger could lock onto the heat exhaust of an aircraft and blow up virtually anything flying below 11,000 feet. Thereafter, I approached several congressmen, politicians, civilians, and audiences at Rotary clubs, universities, and everywhere else I was invited to speak, to make my case for acquiring Stinger missiles for Afghanistan. I urged everyone to relay this message, so that it could reach the top levels of the Reagan administration for serious consideration.

My urgency and perseverance paid off. Three senators, Charlie Wilson of Texas (famously played by Tom Hanks in the 2007 movie *Charlie Wilson's War*), Gordon J. Humphrey of New Hampshire, and my newfound friend Don Ritter of Pennsylvania took up the cause and pushed for the US government's approval to deliver the Stingers to the freedom fighters.

This was allegedly done against the wishes of Secretary of State George Schultz, Secretary of Defense Caspar Weinberger, and US Ambassador to Pakistan Robert Oakley. They feared that the freedom fighters would use the Stingers against US interests. Their concerns were never realized.

Once the Stingers got into the hands of the freedom fighters it did not take them long to perfect their aim. Down came the Hind 17s and 24s and MiGS. According to reports, the freedom fighters had a better than 60 percent kill rate. The threat of the assault helicopters disappeared and the MiGs could no longer fly low enough to drop their bombs. Those that they did drop were from such a high elevation that they missed their targets. In 1988, with the Soviet air power nullified, the war was over and the Red Army was ousted from Afghanistan.

Due to President Reagan's commitment to peace, perseverance against communism, and assistance to the people of Afghanistan, and also the valor and bravery of the Afghan freedom fighters, the Red Army was defeated in Afghanistan. As a result, the days were numbered for the rest of the communist empire. After Afghanistan, worldwide communism fell like a house of cards.

Thank you, Mr. Reagan. We enjoyed our partnership with you. The free world owes you a great deal.

After the defeat of the Red Army, Afghans all over the world were rejoicing. I started making immediate plans to go back home, but unfortunately it was not to be. Soon after the defeat of the Red Army, the US, under President George H. W. Bush, stood aside to allow the leaders of the freedom fighters decide the future of their nation.

Instead of joining forces to help heal the wounds of Afghanistan, the freedom fighters broke along ethnic groups and began fighting one another. The bloodbath that resulted from this infighting far surpassed the blood that was spilt during the Soviet invasion.

The city of Kabul became divided into separate sections based on ethnicity. Citizens could not travel from one section to the other without proper papers. Gulbuddin Hekmatyar, the leader of the Hezb e Islami, (Islamic Party) who was appointed prime minister under the newly selected President Burhanuddin Rabbani, stationed himself outside of Kabul and rained thousands of rockets upon the city on a daily basis. In short, more than 60 percent of the city of Kabul was destroyed and thousands of citizens killed.

This turn of events distressed me to the point that I washed my hands of Afghanistan in disgust and turned my full attention to my work and family.

////////////

President Bush got involved in Iraq after that country invaded Kuwait, and Afghanistan was put on the back burner of U.S. foreign policy. With US interests diverted away from Afghanistan, the country was being destroyed region by region, village by village, province by province. The major destruction occurred in Kabul. Among the buildings destroyed were two of our family's historic palaces of Darul Aman and Tapay Tajbeg, built during my Uncle King Amanullah's reign. The main palace, which was built during my great-grandfather King Abdurrahman's reign, and which he funded out of his pocket, also received a great deal of damage.

The central government of Afghanistan ceased to exist. Historically, the tribes of Afghanistan rallied around a strong leader, never around a policy. Thus, a king who was considered the shadow of Allah on earth wielded a great deal of power. When the king and his cousin Daoud were removed from power and the Soviet Union invaded Afghanistan, the power of the central government was destroyed. Without a central power as established by King Abdurrahman in 1880, the tribes rallied around their respective strongmen. The Hazara tribe rallied around Mazari, Mohaqiq, and Khalili, their strong leaders. The Tajek tribe rallied around their strong man, Massoud. The Uzbek tribe rallied around Dostum. The Pushtoons, the largest of the tribes, did not have any strong man to rally around, but their common language and code of ethics–the Pushtoonwali code—kept them together.

The Pakistanis needed the Pushtoons, as they had been the warriors throughout Afghanistan's turbulent history. In 1996, they came up with the idea of bringing Mullah Omar, a one-eyed illiterate Pakistani Pushtoon, and about 40 others out of Afghanistan's border town of Spin Boldak in the Kandahar province carrying Qurans. The group stated that that they were the followers of Islam and supporters of King Mohammed Zahir Shah (my cousin and the last king, who ruled from 1933 until he was ousted in 1973), and that they wanted to bring peace to the country.

The people were tired of fighting and when they saw these Taliban (religious students), they put down their guns. The Pakistanis knew that Omar had no power or credentials, so to correct the situation, they took Omar to the mosque in Kandahar that housed the cape of Mohammad (PBUH), a famous holy relic. They put the cape on his shoulders and gave him the title of Amir ul Momeneen (the leader of Islam). Through this unholy act, they managed to give this one-eyed bandit the power to be able to unite the Pushtoons. After this, they put Omar on an ivory tower to keep him out of reach, for they knew that if the Afghans got close to him they would see through the guise.

At this time Rabbani was the president of Afghanistan, and Ahmad Shah Massoud (referred to by the French as the Lion of Panjsheer) was the minister of defense.

After taking control of Kandahar without a fight, Mullah Omar and his gang continued their progress and went to Herat. After delivering the message of peace to other regions in the South and Southeast, they arrived in Kabul. President Rabbani and Massoud abandoned the capital and escaped north to Mazar-e-Sharif, the fourth largest city in the country, which had resisted the Taliban encroachment. The 3,000-meter-high Salang Tunnel in the Hindukush Mountains, built by the Russians in the 1960s, was a natural defense line for the northern provinces.

By now the group's attempt to subdue region after region brought to light the real intent of the Taliban. They were not the soldiers of Allah, nor the representatives of King Zahir Shah. They were the tools of Pakistan and its Inter-Services Intelligence (ISI) to control Afghanistan.

The North could not be penetrated by the existing number of the Taliban. Dostum, an Uzbek, and Malik, a Tajek, both of whom had assumed the titles of generals, formed an alliance among their fighters to defend the North. The Tajek tribal leader Massoud and some of followers had retreated to the far North to an area called Khoja Bowedeen, near the Uzbekistan border.

The Taliban needed more fighters. In order to give Mullah Omar support, Pakistan's ISI invited Osama bin Laden to go to Afghanistan. Osama accepted the offer happily as he was about to be thrown out of Sudan. A very rich man, bin Laden entered Afghanistan with plenty of his own money and the support of Saudi Prince Sheikh Turkie and thousands of Arab fighters. To tighten the bond between himself and Omar, he married one of Omar's daughters. Thus Al Qaida was born in Afghanistan, where the plans for bombing the US embassies in Africa and later, the destruction of the World Trade Center in New York, were planned and carried out.

During the Clinton administration, nothing was done to curtail the reappearance of the Taliban and the establishment of the Al Qaida bases in Afghanistan. The ISI was working very closely with bin Laden on attempting to subdue the country, and it was Pakistani Prime Minister Nawaz Sharif's dream to destroy Afghanistan's military and civilian sectors to the point of no return. And he succeeded. In fact, he boasted about this in front of the Pakistani parliament when he was removed from office by General Musharraf, who thereafter assumed the Presidency of Pakistan. In Afghanistan, Nawaz is known as the father of the Taliban and Benazir Bhutto, as its mother.

Upon the emergence of the Taliban on the Afghan scene in 1996, I once again started my active participation in the affairs of Afghanistan. I traveled to different corners of the United States, gave talks and newspaper interviews, and appeared on national television to warn the public about the dangers that this new threat posed for us all.

During a trip to Washington at this time to visit US Representative Dana Rohrabacher of California, I ran into my friend Don Ritter, the former senator from Pennsylvania. He greeted me cordially and asked to visit him at the office of the Afghanistan-American Foundation (AAF), which he had established. The foundation office was located across the street from the Capitol Building, and I went to see him the following day. Don asked me if I wanted to join the organization as a board member, which already included some real political heavyweights like former National Security Advisor Zibignew Brzezinski; Zalmai Khalilzad, who would later serve three posts as the US Ambassador to Afghanistan, Iraq, and the United Nations; a number of current and retired US senators; and Afghans such as Qayum Karzai, a restaurateur and brother of Hamed Karzai, and Habib Mayar, president of the New York Afghan Coalition. I was very happy to be invited to be part of such an august body of members, and I happily accepted.

The AAF was working on behalf of Afghanistan and its people. Senator Ritter used his influence within the US Congress to push for funds and other types of assistance for the country, including playing a major role in getting the Stinger missiles to the freedom fighters. Since the foundation depended on financial donations, my board assignment was to try to raise funds for our operations. My strategy was to invite some of my friends whom I considered potentially strong financial supporters to join the board. These included Mike Jones, my fraternity brother from the University of Connecticut; Robert "Shell" Evans, Chairman of the Crane Corporation; and my cousin Afzal Aslami, President of FiberCore, Inc. and Allied Controls. At our first board meeting, it was agreed that Senator Ritter would be the AFF chairman and Shell Evans the president.

The main thrust of AAF's work was to get the US government's help in ridding Afghanistan of the Osama bin Laden hordes and foreign

Talibs who had poured into the country from as far off as Sudan, Saudi Arabia, Chechnya, Pakistan, and Uzbekistan, to name a few. But we could not convince the Clinton administration of the dangers that these people posed for the world at large.

In 1997, I attended several meetings at the US State Department set up by Senator Ritter. One meeting consisted of talks between my cousin Prince Sultan Mahmood Ghazi, the Under Secretary of State, Ms. Robin Raphael, and me. We had scheduled the meeting to ask for US assistance against the Pakistani government interference and their support of the Pakistani Taliban and Osama bin Laden and his militias. Ms. Raphael invited two young men representing the Afghan and Pakistan desks at the State Department to join the meeting. Since my cousin's knowledge of the English language was limited, as he was educated in France, I offered to translate what was discussed.

During the meeting it became apparent to me that Ms. Raphael and the two young representatives were siding more with the Pakistan government. I became very agitated as I informed her that Pakistan was not only supplying arms and ammunition to Al Qaida, but also fuel. I further explained that Osama was operating two heroin manufacturing laboratories inside Afghanistan, supported by the ISI, and was using the funds earned to set up his training camps within Afghanistan. I continued to say that should the US not take action against what was happening to and within Afghanistan, the end result would be disastrous not only for the region, but for the world.

All three—Ms. Raphael and the two representatives—vehemently denied my remarks and said that such things were not happening and Pakistan was not involved. We left in utter disappointment.

Once again, as with our meeting with Senator Church's aide in which we warned her about losing Iran if they disregarded Afghanistan, our predictions came true. This time, however, disregarding our warnings would result in a much worse scenario.

During this time, while working on Afghanistan affairs, I was also very involved with our fiber optic projects. FiberCore, Inc., Afzal's company where I worked as the vice president of marketing, had acquired a fiber manufacturing company in Jena, a city in the former East Germany. Since the worldwide fiber optic market was very strong, FiberCore not only expanded its operations in Jena, but also entered into a joint venture agreement with a group of Saudi businessmen and opened a manufacturing plant in Riyadh.

It was interesting to note that during this period, when Al Qaeda and the Taliban were settled in Kandahar as their base, an American oil company out of California by the name of UNOCAL established an office in Kandahar and put an American as its head. Ambassador Robert Oakley's wife was allegedly also a high official of UNOCAL. The company was very interested in running a gas pipeline from Turkmenistan to Pakistan via the territory under the control of Al Qaeda/Taliban. To do this, they needed the support of these terrorist groups. So to appease the leadership, UNOCAL invited a group of the Taliban to the United States. They wined and dined them in Texas and California.

At the same time, a Saudi Prince by the name of Sheikh Turkie, who was the cousin of King Fahd of Saudi Arabia and also the kingdom's head of intelligence services, opened his own oil company, Delta, in Kandahar. Like all Saudis, Turkie was a staunch Wahabi, (an ultra anti-Islamic conservative sect). He supported the Taliban and Al Qaeda financially and he was also vying for the gas pipe line with the Turkmenistan government. Since his direct influence over Al Qaeda and the Taliban was strong, UNOCAL could not compete against Delta and thus closed its operations.

In August of 1998, when the Taliban made a final successful attack on the North and conquered Mazar-I-Sharif and all provinces in the North, Sheikh Turkie flew to Kandahar to congratulate the Taliban and Al Qaeda for their victory. This move on Turkic's part angered me greatly and convinced me once and for all that the Arabs were behind the Al Qaeda/Taliban movements in Afghanistan. But then I should not have been surprised, because when the Taliban announced their government in Afghanistan, they received recognition from only three countries in the world: Pakistan, the United Arab Emirates, and Saudi Arabia.

In 1999, the FiberCore, Inc. board agreed to seek out the possibility of setting up an optical fiber manufacturing facility in Cairo, Egypt. As the VP of Marketing and Sales, it was my responsibility to set up the necessary appointments with our potential Egyptian partners. On this trip I was accompanied by my cousin and the company president, Afzal Aslami, and a very beautiful Afghan/Russian lady by the name of Marianne Zamayar. Her father was from Afghanistan and her mother from Azerbaijan, a former Russian republic. Since her company represented our products, I deemed it necessary that she should accompany us as a member of our team. Her very presence, beauty, and elegance and her knowledge in the field of electronics enhanced our business presentation to the Egyptian investors. She was a definite asset, even before I was aware of the important role that she would play in solidifying my suspicions of Sheik Turkie.

Upon our arrival in Cairo we checked in at the Nile Hilton. This was a magnificent hotel, situated on the banks of the Nile River. At the reception desk, I requested rooms on the twenty-fifth floor, as that had a great unencumbered view of the city. I was told that we could not have rooms on that floor because the twenty-fifth to twenty-eighth floors were occupied by a Saudi Prince, Sheikh Turkie, and his family. I was dumbfounded. I could not believe that my nemesis, the one who openly supported the terror groups in my homeland, was residing in the same hotel.

I requested rooms closest to the floors occupied by Turkie. I wanted a chance to either run into him or at least make him aware of my presence. We were given rooms on the twenty-fourth floor.

On one occasion, after finishing a meeting I returned to join Marianne, to whom I referred as Dukhtar-e-Afghan, "Afghan girl," for lunch at the hotel swimming pool. It was a hot August day and with my jacket over one shoulder, I arrived at the pool to find Marianne wearing a very provocative pink bikini, which complemented every beautiful curve of her body. Lying on a chaise lounge with her long black hair flowing over the back of the chair, she was surrounded by four young men of different origins.

As I walked towards her, she raised her finely manicured hand and waved to me. Her Versace sunglasses hid her beautiful dark eyes, but when I arrived at her side she removed her glasses, flashed me a bright smile, and referring to me as His Highness Prince Ali Seraj of Afghanistan, introduced me to her entourage of admirers. She then introduced them to me as the bodyguards of Sheikh Turkie. When I heard his name, I muttered that he was my nemesis. I noticed the four men tense up, look at one another, and then move quickly to stand between me and a group of children who were swimming at the shallow end of the pool.

I was amused at their reaction for they obviously thought that as an Afghan, whose country was being devastated by those supported by Turkie, I presented a real danger to the sheikh's offspring. Nevertheless, I shook each of their hands and asked them to extend my greetings to Sheikh Turkie. I was sure that they would convey my message to the Sheikh, or at least apprise him that I way staying one floor below him.

Marianne later informed me that the bodyguards came from different European countries, and one was a Russian. I was very happy about my decision to bring Marianne with us. She accomplished with a smile what I would not have been able to do—attract the attention of the supporter of the killers of my people and maybe make him a little bit concerned about my being there.

After that day, anytime I came to the pool the body guards would usher the kids in one corner of the pool. It made me happy to know that they feared me.

Whether the Sheikh considered me a threat or it was time for him to leave, I was frustrated to learn one morning that he and his entourage had departed. Soon after that we left without signing an agreement with the Egyptians.

As it so happened, Al Qaida bombed the U.S. embassies in Kenya and Dar es Salaam, Africa. President Bill Clinton's reaction to this murderous act was to send a naval ship to the Indian Ocean near Pakistan and launch several cruise missiles on Osama's camp in southern Afghanistan. As the missiles were about to go over the Pakistani airspace, the US informed the Pakistanis of their plan. Before the missiles could reach the camp, bin Laden was warned by the Pakistani ISI to vacate. The missiles destroyed an empty camp. Bin Laden was having tea in another area.

Feeling disillusioned at the laissez-faire attitude of the Clinton administration, I spent less time on Afghanistan and more on FiberCore, Inc. Afzal Aslami was fully involved in the fiber optic business, and in addition to his purchase of the plant in Germany and establishment of a joint venture company for fiber production in Saudi Arabia, we purchased a patent from Russian scientists to produce synthetic glass using plasma technology. While overseeing these operations, I came across a fiber optic production facility called Xtal located in Campinas, Brazil. Afzal Aslami and I went to Brazil to finalize the purchase.

Since I was responsible for locating and negotiating the transaction, I was put in charge of overseeing the operations there.

Xtal was the highlight of my business career. I obtained a beautiful 10,000-square-foot mansion situated on twenty acres of pristine land in a gated community. The house contained four individual bedroom suites and came with a large swimming pool, outdoor wet bar, tennis court, and complete Brazilian-style barbeque terrace. A full-sized soccer field stood down the hill from the tennis court. Fruit and mango trees grew all around the estate.

Because of the security situation in Brazil, especially pertaining to kidnappings, the gated community was surrounded by a high wall with an electric fence. Thirty fully armed guards kept an eye on the 240 mansions within this compound. I was advised to change my travel routes to our factory on a daily basis and to change cars at least once a week. I did as advised, but after a couple of months I got tired of driving in a small Corolla. Against my secretary Diana Chefen's advice, I ordered the factory to have a Mitsubishi Jeep delivered to my house.

The day the Jeep arrived, Diana was at my house for some work, so I asked her to follow me as I drove out of the compound. It felt amazing to be behind the wheel of such a great piece of machinery. Just after cruising onto the highway I heard sirens, and looking into the rearview mirror I found a police car on my tail. I pulled over, and holding my Connecticut driver's license and US passport in my hand, waited for the police officer to walk over. Since I could not speak any Portuguese at the time, I asked Diana, who had stopped her car behind mine, to translate.

The two officers looked at my passport, talked to each other, and then said that my license was not valid for driving in Brazil. I told them that the Brazilian Consulate in New York had told me it was valid. We went on back and forth for over an hour. Finally they pulled out a regulation book, and luckily Diana found the part that it stated the validity of US licenses in Brazil.

Satisfied, they saluted me, and as they were about to leave I told Diana to ask them why they had stopped me as I had not broken any traffic laws. They smiled and said that they stopped me because of my car. They said that only drug dealers drove such cars.

I then realized why all the wealthy people in Brazil drove old cars. When I got to the factory, I instructed Diana to send the car back to the dealer and bring me a Corolla.

At Xtal I was in charge of over 500 employees, and I found the Brazilian people extremely kind and friendly. As much as I loved Brazil and its people, my heart was still with Afghanistan, so I traveled to the US as often as I could to continue my work for my people. Afzal, being a cousin and an Afghan who also cared deeply about his home country, was supportive of my efforts.

Since the Afghanistan-American Foundation was not receiving any assistance from the Clinton administration, we decided to carry our message to the US Congress. On one of my trips to the US the AAF decided to go on a hunger strike on the steps of the US Capitol. A young intern, Yaqoub, working as the AAF office manager, was tasked with calling several Afghans from various states to participate.

I financed the rental of tents to be set up on the Capitol grounds and Yaqoub got the necessary permits to allow us to follow through with our plans. The hunger strike date was set for the first week of April, 1999. The Afghan community representative from New York, Habib Mayar, arrived a day before the event. We prepared signs stating that we would not move and would not eat until the US government heeded our pleas to save Afghanistan. Other colorful signs called for Pakistan to get out and other sayings.

We pitched the tents a day before the hunger strike. I woke up early on day one because I planned to pick up Yaqoub from the office. I put on my calf-length black leather overcoat and went out to catch a cab. Once outside I caught a gust of bitter cold wind and rain on my face. Luck was not with us. Nevertheless, I was intent on going through with our resolve, good weather or bad. I picked up Yaqoub and drove to the Capitol. After parking the car, we walked up the steps where the signs had been posted. We were excited, expecting to find throngs of Afghans, and raced up the steps. When we got to the terrace where we were going to hold TV interviews, we were totally amazed at what we saw. Instead of crowds of Afghans, there was only Habib Mayar, head of the New York Afghan Coalition, dressed in the traditional Afghan payran/tumban outfit of baggy pants with a long shirt going past the knees. On his head he wore a round Nooristan cap which had become popular by the Afghan freedom fighters during the war with the Soviet Red Army.

The weather was cold and wet. Habib shivered in his thin outfit and Yaqoub's business suit was getting drenched. My very expensive leather coat was stretching down to my ankles. Not wanting my two faithful and dedicated Afghans to catch pneumonia, I drove to the nearest shop and bought raincoats, socks, and blankets. By the time I got back, Habib's lips were blue from the cold and he was talking to a young Afghan girl and her male friend, who had braved the weather, and the Ariana Afghan TV reporter Nabil Muskinyar. I stayed away from the interview as I was totally disgusted and disappointed at my fellow Afghans' response to what some of us thought was a crucial plan of action.

Standing there on the steps, getting soaked and feeling miserable, a Capitol policeman who had been watching us from his very dry and likely warm room approached us. In a sympathetic tone of voice, he asked us to go under the terrace to get out of the rain. The three of us in one voice said that we would not move as we did not want to miss the congressional members leaving the building. The guard looked at us with sad eyes and told us that we were standing on the wrong side of the Capitol. He informed us that the congressmen and women came out from the opposite side. I looked at Yaqoub in anger, for he was the one who had arranged the place, and he sheepishly avoided my cold stare.

By now it was too late to do anything. Our signs were all washed out, we were drenched to the bone, and except for us three, and there were no other Afghans. So, with broken spirits we gathered up everything we had brought, called the rental company to pick up the tents, and went back to the AAF office to get dry. When we got there and listened to the messages, we found out to our dismay that Afghans had come to the Capitol, on the right side, and not seeing any activity, had left.

Our hunger strike plans went down the drain as Afghanistan descended into chaos. Having failed in our hunger strike plan, I returned to Brazil and paradise.

/////////

Robin Raphael was replaced by Karl Inderfurth at the State Department. Upon assuming the position, he called for a meeting of certain members of congress, State Department officials, Carl Richardson (later to become the governor of New Mexico), and Afghan community representatives including me and Hassan Noori, an Afghan community leader from California. I flew back to Washington and looked forward to meeting the new undersecretary.

We met in Mr. Inderfurth's conference room. I was seated between California Congressmen Dana Rohrabacher and Ed Royce, longtime friends of Afghanistan, and directly across the table from Mr. Inderfurth. The purpose of the meeting was to discuss the possibility of bringing peace to Afghanistan through a two-plus-six plan. This plan would involve setting up a peace conference between Russia and the United States as the two main powers along with the six Central Asian countries of Afghanistan, Iran, Pakistan, Tajikistan, Uzbekistan, and Turkmenistan.

In order for this plan to materialize, Mr. Inderfurth stated that he would send Mr. Richardson to Islamabad (Pakistan) and Kabul to promote the idea. I argued that the plan was not going to succeed because Nawaz Sharif, the deposed Prime Minister of Pakistan, who was considered the father of the Taliban, prided himself on destroying Afghanistan's military and civilian sectors to the point of no return, and he was supported in this venture by the Pakistani ISI. I also noted that he had made this statement in front of the Pakistan Parliament before leaving office. I said that peace would not come to Afghanistan as long as the ISI ruled Pakistan.

The only person around the table who took an interest in what I said was Congressman Royce. He even wrote down my statements in his notebook. Everyone else disregarded it. Once again, my prediction was right.

Mr. Richardson did go to Pakistan and Afghanistan, and upon his return the New York Times printed a front-page photo of him embracing an old, white-bearded Afghan man with a caption stating that the old man was the gardener at the US Embassy in Kabul. Mr. Richardson praised the good work he was doing keeping the gardens beautiful and well kept.

So much for the two-plus-six plan. The issue was never raised again.

//////////

Chalking up the State Department experience as another failure, I returned to Brazil, this time to stay for good, or so I thought. We had started an $80 million expansion program at Xtal, and this needed my undivided attention.

In spite of long work days and endless details, try as I might, I could not get Afghanistan out of my mind. I believed very strongly in re-establishing the monarchy in my home country. The people of Afghanistan wanted the monarchy. King Mohammad Zahir Shah was in exile in Rome with his immediate family, and even though his father took the throne in the name of my uncle King Amanullah and proclaimed himself king in 1929, I did not feel animosity towards him. He was still a cousin, part of my royal family, and as a former reigning king and elder statesman, I believed that he could unite the different tribes and thus bring peace to the country.

When I finally made another trip to the US, I relayed this message to every contact I had in Washington. At last, in the spring of 1999, 12 members of the US Congress—10 Republicans and 2 Democrats—extended a written invitation to King Mohammad Zahir Shah to visit the United States and meet with them. I submitted this invitation to the king's office in Rome. The response did not come until two months and many phone calls later. When it finally did, it was not what the congressmen expected. The king stated in his letter that he was too busy and would come at a more appropriate time. When I delivered this letter to those who had extended the invitation, I was told to tell the ex-king that his response was last nail that he had driven in the coffin of Afghanistan.

This action by King Zahir Shah put out the flicker of light that was still shining for Afghanistan. The only hope left for the return of the monarchy was my cousin, Sultan Mahmood Ghazi. He was my first cousin from his mother's side and therefore a nephew of King Amanullah and first cousin of King Zahir Shah on his father's side. Since the people of Afghanistan still held extremely high respect for King Amanullah as well as King Zahir Shah, Sultan Mahmood, having a connection to both, stood a very good chance of becoming the next king.

I discussed this idea with some members of the AAF and it was decided that I, Qayum Karzai (brother of Hamid Karzai, later President of Afghanistan), and Habib Mayar would visit Prince Sultan Mahmood at his residence in Alexandria, Virginia. At this time most of the members of both royal houses of Afghanistan lived in and around Washington, DC. When we presented him with our proposal, he paused in deep thought for a few minutes. He then asked us to give him two weeks to decide.

Two weeks later the prince called and asked to see me. He came to my hotel room, sat down by the window, looked outside, and asked me if I could see any stars. I was confused by his question and told him that it was a bright day with the sun shining. It was not possible to see the stars. He said that so long as the sun was shining, one could not see the stars, and in the same way, so long as King Zahir was alive, no one from his side of the family could step up to take his place.

I was disappointed at his decision. The king was in his eighties and not long for this world, while Sultan was in his seventies. He was young enough to have a positive effect on the political outcome in Afghanistan. But it was not to be.

I shared this message with our community, and we decided to wait and see who would become the next president of the United States before making any new plans. The two candidates were George W. Bush an Al Gore. Since we had had better working relationships under republican administrations, including the Reagan era, we hoped that the Texan would win the election.

CHAPTER 15

THE TALIBAN THREAT AND GEORGE W. BUSH

I was in Brazil when I heard that George W. Bush had won the election. I was elated. Upon his inauguration, I and a number of Afghan community members sent Mr. Bush our congratulations and waited to see what he would do for Afghanistan.

By year 2000, the Taliban/Al Qaida was becoming more vicious and daring by the day. Public executions, cutting off of hands, and the stoning of women became a common daily routine of the Taliban governance. Closing down girls' schools; shutting down the media, music, and entertainment; and locking women behind closed doors had become a common policy since the outset of the Taliban regime. They even banned kite flying, a favorite pastime of young Afghan boys.

I came back to the US in June 2001 as my daughter Sahar would be getting married to Jonathan Ross-Wiley on September 1 of that year. When I was last home in Milford, Connecticut, Sahar brought Jon home to introduce him to the family. She was slightly nervous because of what had happened the last time she brought a young man home. I remembered the day clearly: a week shy of becoming sixteen, she came to ask me if she could go out to the movies with a young man from her school. I was busy working on something and said yes. Later, when Beth made me realize what I had agreed to, I was very concerned. But I could not take back my word. Instead, I went up to my room, changed into my Afghan clothes, and put on a turban. Back downstairs, I took down the antique Afghan sword and shield that hung on the wall and sat at the door waiting for the young man to arrive, much to my daughter 's objections. When the young man entered the house and saw me sitting there, he went pale. He could hardly get a "Hello, sir," out of his mouth. Sahar grabbed his hand ushered him out of the house, but not before he heard my gruff voice tell him to make sure that she was home by 11:00 pm. Needless to say, he brought her home at 10:00 pm and never showed up again.

I was quite strict with the upbringing of my three daughters. I decided from the time they were knee high that they were going to be raised under Afghan discipline, like I was. No dating, makeup, or long earrings until the age of sixteen. While they could go out as a group, there had to be a chaperone on hand. I was raising three princesses, and they represented our family and royal heritage. Any wrongdoing on their part would tarnish the name of our family, so it was important that they be brought up to make the right choices in their lives. My responsibility was to love and protect them and to make sure that they had a good education and made the right choice when the time came for them to get married. I always emphasized education and told them that they should depend on themselves first before depending on their husbands.

While my daughters were growing up I told them stories about Queen Soraya, the wife of my uncle, King Amanullah, who modernized Afghanistan during his reign from 1919 to 1929. A member of the Tarzi family, Queen Soraya was a bold and colorful figure who made her mark in history with her actions on behalf of women's rights. She sent Afghani women to college for the first time, inspired women to get involved in the country's development, launched Afghanistan's first women's magazine, encouraged girls to go to school, and appeared in public without the veil. My daughters learned to be proud of Queen Soraya, and they took this heritage and my advice to heart. Sahar earned a Master of Science in genetics, Alia got her B.A. from Emerson College in Boston and her M.A. in International Business, and Safia received a degree in environmental sciences. All three were gainfully employed in well-paid jobs before they got married.

My first-born, my beautiful Princess Sahar, made the right choice with Jonathan Ross-Wiley. I liked him the minute I met him. He had had a good upbringing and education and was well spoken, so when Sahar asked for my permission to marry him, I had no problem in giving her my blessing.

When Jonathan formally asked me for my daughter's hand in marriage, I put my hand on his shoulder and asked him if he liked vodka. He said yes. I then led him to the bar, poured two glasses, and we drank to his and Sahar's health and happiness.

Since our first child was getting married, Maribeth did not spare any expense. First, she hired a wedding planner to arrange everything. I was told that the first planning meeting was very important and that I should be there, as my opinion and involvement was very crucial to the happy event. So I rushed home from Brazil for this most important meeting. Never having met a wedding planner before, I put on my best attire and greeted her when she came into our home. Maribeth, Sahar, the wedding planner, and I sat down around the dining room table. The planner looked at me and asked about the budget for the wedding. "Whatever it takes," I said, and thereafter I ceased to exist as far as she was concerned. The next time I saw her was at the wedding.

I must admit that both Sahar and Beth made an excellent choice in selecting this wedding planner. Every detail was impeccable, starting with the pristine venue, the Water's Edge on Long Island Sound, where the wedding hall was elegantly covered with white roses. Among the approximately 300 guests were my mother and sister, who arrived from Alexandria, Virginia, and my brother and his wife Rona from California. Other relatives came from as far away as California, Washington, DC, New York, and Europe.

The ceremony included both American and traditional Afghan wedding vows, the latter performed by my cousin, Wali Sherzai. As I walked my daughter down the aisle, stepping through mounds of rose petals, I was a very proud man. I had raised Sahar and her sisters well, and everyone who knew them held them in high regard. Looking at the happy smile on my daughter's face, I silently agreed that the whole affair was worth the small fortune it cost, including the complete renovation of the kitchen and the garden at our house.

Sahar and Jonathan left for their honeymoon on September 9, 2001.

//////////

SEPTEMBER 11, 2001

The last of the wedding guests had returned to wherever they came from and I was getting ready to fly back to Brazil. On the morning of September 11, 2001, I had just stepped out of the shower when the phone rang. I picked up the phone and heard my daughter Alia yelling at me to turn on the TV. I quickly switched it on to see an image of smoke coming out of one of the World Trade Center towers. The reporter said that a plane had smashed into the tower. As I watched the live broadcast, I saw a plane fly past the burning building and then a ball of fire and smoke stream out of the second building as it smashed into it from behind. I could not believe my eyes.

I was glued to the TV, listening to the news broadcast about two planes hitting the two towers of the World Trade Center. Then they interrupted to report about another plane hitting the Pentagon and one going down in the woods in Pennsylvania. I watched in disbelief as the two towers came tumbling down in a cloud of dust and smoke.

When they later announced that Al Qaida members were involved in hijacking the planes and that more than 3,000 people were killed because of their murderous deeds, I wondered how the United States would react against these terrorists. On the day after the attack, President Bush visited the World Trade Center and spoke about going after the instigators. I knew that he was going to send troops into Afghanistan.

On September 17, 2001, I sent a four-page letter to President Bush, outlining 13 points that the US must take in order to kill the dragon with the thousand heads. By September 25, 2001, the president responded to me in his own handwriting, commenting about the excellent points I had made and that he would keep in mind.

After receiving his response, I went back to Brazil and my job at Xtal.

As I had anticipated, the US struck the Taliban and Al Qaida in October 2001, and after a month-long series of air strikes by the US-led coalition forces, Afghanistan was purged of the extremist Taliban regime and their terrorist lodgers. The armed coalition forces, backed by the Afghan freedom fighters, destroyed the terrorists' bases and drove them and their Pakistani backers out of Afghanistan. In one phase of these attacks, the Taliban residing in Kabul were surrounded by the freedom fighters. Since they had no place to hide, some of them ran to the woods of Shar-e Naw Park and climbed up the tall evergreens, thinking that no one would see them. The freedom fighters tracked them down and picked them off one by one, shooting them down from the trees.

On November 16, 2001, Kabul was liberated. Germany then hosted a conference in Bonn to determine the make-up of an interim government for Afghanistan. The international community rallied in Japan to pledge monetary assistance toward the reconstruction of the war-torn country. At the meeting in Bonn it was decided that Afghanistan would be a democracy and named Hamid Karzai as the country's first interim president. Karzai was an Afghan freedom fighter and member of the Pushtoon tribe, the largest tribe in Afghanistan.

In December I was informed that the United States Agency for International Development (USAID) was scheduling a meeting that month for the Afghan diaspora to discuss multifaceted economic development for the newly democratic Afghanistan. They were looking for Afghan-Americans with expertise in various fields. On December 15, 2001, I closed up my house in Campinas, Brazil, and told my crew that I would be back in two weeks.

When I arrived in Connecticut, I contacted my cousin Afzal Aslami and we decided to travel together to the meeting in Washington. When we arrived, we found ourselves among about twenty other Afghan-Americans as well as members of USAID, the Overseas Private Investment Corporation (OPIC), the World Bank, US State Department, and others. The Afghans represented fields such as banking, agriculture, engineering, road construction, and telecommunications. Each Afghan gave a presentation about what he expected to bring to the country, and the most important points of discussion were in banking and telecommunications. Noor Dilawari, a banking expert from California, gave a very impressive talk about what was needed to establish a new banking system in Afghanistan and how he was going to resolve the challenges of the process. Afzal and I made a presentation about fiber optics, outlining how FiberCore, Inc., would bring in the world's finest mobile telephone company, including the construction of a fiber optic ring cable that would eventually connect every village, town, and city in Afghanistan.

After everyone completed their presentations, one of the OPIC representatives praised Afzal and me on our telecommunications proposal and said that OPIC would be interested in funding such a project, subject to our business plan. Soon after returning to Connecticut from the meeting, Afzal prepared the business plan and we submitted it to OPIC.

While still in Washington, George Mason University invited me to give a talk on Afghanistan. I asked Afzal to join me, and I presented a very detailed talk on the past and future of Afghanistan. The audience was made up of GMU students and faculty, Afghan-Americans, members of the public, and—seated in the front row—the Afghan government's newly appointed chargé d'affaires to the United States, Mr. Haroon Amin.

After my talk, Mr. Amin and his secretary, Adlay English, came over to thank me and also ask for assistance in finding a facility for the Afghan Embassy, as the old embassy was in need of renovation and could not be occupied. I introduced them to Afzal, and when I relayed Amin's request to him, he asked me to look around Washington for an appropriate location. During my time working in real estate I had made several contacts among property owners in Washington. I called one of them and asked for space. Within one day he had assigned five rooms to the Afghan Embassy within a beautiful building on Sixteenth Street. Mr. Amin was very pleased with my choice, and since the embassy did not yet have a budget, Afzal and I agreed to pay the rent for six months, totaling some sixty thousand dollars, out of our own pockets.

After signing the rental contract, I left for Connecticut to make preparations to leave for Afghanistan to meet with the government about our telecommunications proposal. Afzal had already left for Massachusetts to do the same. We were to meet in Kabul, as I was going to Afghanistan via Delhi and he via Dubai.

Maribeth joined me for the initial India leg of the trip. Since the situation in Afghanistan was uncertain, we decided that she would only accompany me as far as Delhi. When we arrived at the Taj Hotel in Delhi, I immediately contacted the office of Afghanistan's national airline, Ariana Afghan Airlines, to reserve a flight to Kabul. I was told that the airline's schedule was very iffy, and that it would probably take about two weeks for the first scheduled flight to Kabul. Since we had time on our hands, we decided to visit the Taj Mahal in Agra. We stayed at the Oberoi Hotel, one of only two seven-star hotels in the world (with Dubai's Burj al Arab) and visited the Taj Mahal, built by a king for the love of a beautiful woman named Noor Jehan (*Light of the World*). After two days of being tourists, we returned to Delhi. Still no Ariana flights. I was getting very frustrated. I then learned that the airlines flights from Dubai were activated, and since Afzal was going to be there anyway, I decided to fly to Dubai to join him. Maribeth took me to airport as she was taking a flight back to the States the next day.

CHAPTER 16

DESTINATION KABUL

After the formation of the democratic government in Afghanistan in December 2001, throngs of refugees from neighboring countries journeyed back to the newly liberated capital. A number of prominent Afghan émigrés who had fled the country after the communist takeover in 1978 also embarked on the voyage home.

I had faith in my instincts. There was never a doubt in my mind that I would, one day return to Afghanistan. My last glimpse of the country was through the grimy rear window of a bus as it jittered across the Pakistani border twenty-three years earlier. I had managed to evade the checkpoints, but it was a bittersweet victory—a sense of relief coupled with a gnawing regret. The closer the bus brought me to safety, the further it took me from the warm womb of my native land. My memory of the receding rocky terrain was hazy, or maybe it was all those exhaust fumes or the hashish-filled air from the dozen hippies smoking in the rear seats. In hindsight, my senses may have been somewhat impaired, but as I looked upon my country fading out in the distance, I could swear I felt my instincts telling me that this would not be the last time. And I had dreamt of my return every day since.

I had never imagined, however, that when this day came my traveling companions would include a hundred or so convicts. In all likelihood they were neither hardened criminals nor terrorists, otherwise they would be bound for Guantanamo Bay in Cuba. Judging by the pitiful look on their faces, I supposed they were merely petty thieves or illegal immigrants who had crept into the United Arab Emirates in search of a better life. After serving time in prison abroad, they were now being sent home to serve the rest of their sentences in Afghan prisons. Still, I thought, I might have to omit this detail when relating the trip to my wife and ailing mother back in Connecticut. They had both been dead-set against my decision to return to Afghanistan—so soon, at least. In my mind, I dubbed the flight *Con Air*. Afzal, my traveling partner, was not too pleased with the name, as he was nervous about traveling with so many prisoners.

A good businessman knows that the opportunity to make "real money" only comes twice: when a country is destroyed, and later, during reconstruction. The warlords made their money fast when Afghanistan was torn apart by civil war. Now the country was a blank slate. Anything and everything would be possible for farsighted businessmen, but the returns would come at a slower pace.

There were eleven non-prisoners on our Ariana flight, including the Afghan minister of communications and a few businessmen and NGO workers. As the aircraft had been specially sent from Kabul to pick up the inmates in Dubai, we eleven passengers were not in a position to complain. The next flight to Kabul would leave in a week, and maybe even later. I had already been delayed in Delhi three weeks before I had heard there were flights from Dubai, so I was simply grateful to be on board.

With its chipped paint, shabby and clunky seats, and dirty interior, the Boeing 727 looked to be in dire need of repairs. No doubt all the passengers were nagged with worry that the poorly maintained relic from the 1960s would fall apart in midair. I had to smile at the thought that it would be funny to have survived the communists, only to crash or be taken hostage by convicts in an Afghan airline as I neared the motherland nearly two-and-a-half decades later!

Afzal turned his face away and shut his eyes. Just a half hour into the two-hour flight, we both felt like we had been in the air for eons. I reached into my carry-on and slipped out a small canister. A few years ago, a cousin had taken a trip to northern Afghanistan for research purposes and I had requested that he bring back a sample of the country's soil for me. Whenever I felt homesick I would sink my fingers into the canister and rub some of the gray dust over my face. I had lived and worked in America for twenty-three years. I was married to an American and had three daughters who never learned to speak Dari, the Afghan version of Farsi. At times, I felt painfully disconnected from my Afghan roots. The dust made me feel close to home.

Afzal woke up with a jolt when an announcement on the intercom stated that we were entering Afghanistan's airspace. I could not make out the terrain because the passengers all leapt from their seats, clapping and embracing each other. The plane nearly jostled. Even the convicts seemed curiously overjoyed. I thought with sadness that these people had nothing to look forward to but another prison cell. I felt my throat swell up. In the midst of the clamour, someone tapped on my shoulder. It was a flight attendant. He said that the captain was aware that I was on board the flight and would be honored if the prince would join him in the cockpit.

I obliged and followed the attendant to the cockpit. Glancing at the gray duct tape holding pieces of the cockpit ceiling together, I felt as though I had stepped into the carcass of an old aircraft that had crashed somewhere in a jungle, decades ago. Captain Saeedi, an old friend from what seemed like a previous life, sat cheerfully in these surroundings, blissfully unaware of how much aeronautical technology had evolved since the 1970s when he had flown the Ariana Boeings through showers of rockets and U.S.-supplied missiles. He was a friend from the past and I was very happy to see him again.

Warmly giving me the traditional Afghan greeting, "*Salam alaykum warahmatu Allah wa barakatuhu*" (Peace be upon you, and may God's blessings be upon you), the captain spoke with a cigarette dangling from the corner of his mouth. In fact, the whole cockpit was full of smoke. He went on to say what a great honor it was for him to fly me back home. He said that the country needed members of our family now more than ever.

My royal lineage had been both a blessing and a curse over the years. At this moment, however, it was no more relevant than the rural backgrounds of some of the other passengers. On their journey to Afghanistan, we all shared a single spirit. Captain Saeedi told me that I would soon be able to see our beloved capital. Smiling sheepishly, he told me that I had the best seat in the house. I was touched by this, but I knew that it would difficult to see anything because the sky was heavily overcast.

Captain Saeedi turned his attention to the panoply of buttons, wires, and gadgets before him. He picked up a receiver to make radio contact with Kabul Airport. The controller advised him not to land in the capital and veer north instead towards Herat or Mazar-I-Sharif. At this moment, the radio cord was accidentally ripped out of its socket. With a disgusted groan, he tried in vain to paste it back without success. Staring at the disconnected radio, I cleared my throat and asked him if there was a problem. He assured me that there was not, but he appeared distracted. I asked him if we were going to land at the national airport as scheduled. Again, he assured me that by Grace of Allah, we would land in Kabul.

The captain was resolute and made good on his word. After circling above the area that I assumed was Kabul, amid turbulence, he found a clearing and merrily announced that he was going to aim for that opening. Before he could dive into the clearing, I got up and excused myself. I did not want to see death from the front row. Thanking the captain, I went back to my seat beside Afzal, tightened my seat belt, and told my companions to do the same. The talent and expertise of Afghan pilots never ceases to amaze me. Captain Saeedi did dive through that narrow opening, and avoiding all the surrounding mountains safely landed the plane on the tarmac at Kabul airport. We taxied alongside the charred remains of several military aircraft—a reminder of times past including Soviet occupation, civil war, and more recently, US carpet bombings of Taliban and Al Qaida installations.

I was among the first to disembark. As soon as I did, I fell to the ground and pressed my lips against the wet tarmac. Home at last.

Two military soldiers rushed to my side and helped me up. The young men were touched by this open display of emotion. As they escorted me toward the airport terminal I pulled out the small bottle of Afghan soil that had given me so much comfort over the years. Now it was time to return what was left back to the motherland. I unscrewed the cap and spread the dust into the air, bidding it a welcome home.

Dazed, I looked around me and tried to connect my surroundings with the images I had stored in my memory. Was this the same airport where I had come countless times to bid farewell to friends or collect visitors, extending greetings from the sun-drenched roof terrace? This airport was a mess of broken windows and scattered debris. Burnt shells of airplanes and helicopters lay in heaps near the runway. Guards toting Kalashnikovs were posted at every corner. It seemed more like a military outpost.

Inside the dimly lit terminal a number of men rushed out of the woodwork to greet the returning guests. They recognized me immediately and marveled at how little I had changed. I figured that that was largely due to the fact that I still had my signature goatee, and that it was still dark brown. They embraced me, kissed my hand, and asked me a myriad of questions. I did not recognize any of them.

Eventually I realized that these were the same men who had staffed the airport 25 years ago. Their faces, tired and weatherbeaten, seemed to bear testament to the hardships they had suffered.

An attendant at the airport collected my suitcase, and as I stepped out of the terminal a driver was waiting to take me, Afzal, and the Afghan communications minister to the Intercontinental Hotel, the only accommodation available for guests of our business and diplomatic stature.

As we had not eaten anything since breakfast in Dubai, we decided to stop at a local restaurant for lunch. Our Land Cruiser circled the town amidst heavy traffic for some time before stopping at the Herat Kebab Shop. Apparently, the owner of the restaurant was a friend of the communications minister, for he immediately escorted us to a private dining room. Looking around, I did not see a single familiar face. Even the restaurant owner was from another province. The streets were full of strangers. Before the disaster that had befallen the nation, every third person was someone I knew. Now I felt like a stranger in my own land.

To the naked eye, the devastation was not as severe as one would have expected. Seeing the city from the vintage point of the restaurant, I noticed that it had not been razed to the ground. Many shops lined the streets and shopkeepers went about their business the way they had twenty-three years ago. Most buildings in this area of the city called Shar-e Now ("New City") were still standing, albeit some were pockmarked by machine guns. My attention was drawn to the cigarette stall at the corner of the park, across the street from the restaurant. That was the stall where my cousin Abdul Kabir bought his cigarettes before being mowed down by the rockets some 25 years ago. It was still there, but sadly, my cousin was not. He had passed away in the US from a heart attack a few years back. I think it was more like a broken heart, as he missed Afghanistan very much. Silently, I whispered a prayer for his soul.

Through the dusty windows of the kebab shop I watched the bearded soldiers in their dirty army fatigues and Kalashnikovs slung over their shoulders. They were enveloped in a cloud of acrid smoke, which every car seemed to emanate. The sight ruined my normally healthy appetite. These soldiers were too young to remember a different Afghanistan. My Afghanistan. Most were not even born when the king was still on the throne. What were they guarding so vigilantly? Was their way of life worth defending? Could they be blamed for not knowing any better?

My thoughts were disturbed as the waiter placed a trayful of delicious smelling lamb kebob skewers on warm flat bread called nan. Another waiter brought bowls of yogurt with chopped cucumbers mixed with dried mint.

The smell of kebobs was overwhelming and I picked several skewers and started pulling chunks of tender meat with pieces of nan. I avoided the yogurt for fear of bacteria. In the olden days, living in Afghanistan, one developed resistance to local germs. Now, however, I did not want to take the chance of contracting what had affectionately been referred to in the old foreigner community as Kabulitis, or KT for short.

After finishing our lamb kebob lunch, we all piled in the Land Cruiser and headed for the former Inter-Continental Hotel, which was situated on a hill on the outskirt of the city. Although no longer an Inter-Continental, it still bore the name. As we reached the main entrance of the hotel, we were greeted by a doorman with a long white beard. His dark face suddenly lit up as he caught sight of me.

"*Oh khodaya shukur kay shumara boz mebinam!*" (Thank Allah that I am once again seeing you) he croaked, and embraced me. I looked at him and tried to remember where and when I had seen him. He realized my confusion and said that he was Khodaidad. Tears streaming down his wrinkly cheeks, the old man fumbled in his tattered *shalwar kameez* and slipped out a faded photograph. He said that he had kept this for more than twenty years. He knew that one day

I would come back. He placed the photo in my hand. It was a picture of me and the doorman, then clean-shaven and garbed in a neat red uniform with shiny gold buttons, standing at precisely the same spot. He had kept his job at the hotel throughout two decades of political upheaval and managed to preserve a relic from days gone by.

I remembered Khodaidad now. And I remembered the day the photo was taken. It was New Year's Eve, 1972. There was a party at the hotel. It was the last time King Zahir Shah, who ruled from 1933 to 1973, would usher in a new year as reigning monarch of Afghanistan. It was also a few months prior to the coup d'état, which led to the demise of our centuries' old dynasty and paved the way for a communist takeover five years later. None of the merry-makers suspected then that it would be decades before Afghans would have cause to celebrate again.

I looked back at the old man's furrowed face and saw little resemblance to the dapper fellow who used to greet me and my guests whenever they came to the hotel for a little diversion. As the old man helped me with my luggage, he wearily related some of the ups and downs he and his colleagues had experienced over the years. The hotel had been reduced to a staff of five. There were nights when they heard rockets flying from their windows. There was the time when the top floor of the hotel caught fire and the staff had to scramble up to put it out. And then that fateful morning when a rocket landed at the entrance door, blowing off the legs of one of the doormen.

It occurred to me that it was I who should be carrying Khodaidad's baggage, and not the other way around. I, as a Prince of Afghanistan, was making my grand comeback to the land of my forefathers, after the Soviet invasion, civil war, Taliban rule, and aerial bombardment. But it was men like Khodaidad who had shown true courage worthy of the great Pushtoon warriors whose blood flowed through my veins.

Khodaidad quickly opened the door and we all went inside the hotel. He followed us and once inside, went up to a man dressed in a three-piece suit, with a full beard standing by the reception desk. The old man whispered in his ear, and the suited man looked directly at me. A broad grin appeared on his face. He walked towards me with outstretched arms and gave me the traditional Afghan greeting of pressing the body three times, once on the right, then on the left and then back on the right. While he was doing this, he kept saying,

"Allah be praised." When he saw the confused look on my face, he told me that he was Dastaghir. I remembered then that he used to be the manager of the Pamir Supper club, a restaurant situated on the top floor of the hotel where Maribeth and I celebrated our wedding reception in 1974 and where I spent most of my weekends dancing the night away. The Pamir was the most popular nightspot in town, after my club, of course. He was now the general manager of the hotel.

The lobby looked the same, but I was told that only two floors were habitable, as the rest of the floors had received severe damage from the rockets and eventual fire. I was given a suite on the second floor, the only one with two bedrooms. The elevators were not working, so Afzal and I walked up two flights of stairs to get to our suite. The rooms were spacious and the floors covered with Afghan carpets. When I pulled open the curtains I found bullet holes in the window glass which had been taped over with masking tape. I turned around and spotted bullet holes in the walls opposite the windows.

My room faced the Bagh-e-Bala Palace, the summer residence of my Great-grandfather Abdurrahman that overlooked the city of Kabul. How peaceful . . . from a distance, one might never know this city had seen the horrors of war. My mind wandered back to my childhood days of folly and *insouciance*. No, it was not a dream . . . it was here that I had spent the best days—and nights—of my life. But was it really so long ago?

When Khodaidad brought in our luggage, I gave him a $100 bill, as I had not yet changed any money, and thanked him, not for his service, but for his courage and what he had endured. He looked at the crisp bill that I had placed in his palm and a broad grin appeared on his crinkled lips, and he gave me another one of his bear hugs. He almost danced out of the room, repeatedly, thanking me for what he called a very handsome gift. Little did I know that the exchange rate of dollars to afghanis was so great that a whole family lived on less per month. After he left, I went downstairs to walk around the lobby and reminisce about the wonderful times we had spent in and around this hotel.

The coffee shop, where I had spent multitude of hours, convening meetings or entertaining friends or just meeting girls, had been turned into a dining room. The kitchen was totally destroyed and food was now cooked on open fires in the back of the hotel. The bar had become a conference room. One remaining gift shop displayed Afghan-style jewelry, lapis lazuli, and artifacts. Without the elevator music that was once piped throughout the lobby, an eerie silence permeated the place.

I asked Dastaghir about the music. He frowned and said that the Taliban had banned all music and destroyed the sound system. I asked if any music shops may have opened since the defeat of the Taliban. He assured me that the day the Taliban were driven out—the very next day—music stores opened up all over Kabul. I was very happy over this news and decided there and then that I was going to bring life back into the hotel.

I returned to our suite, took a cold shower (since there was no hot water), changed my clothes, and went downstairs to check on some of the other guests and change some money. After giving the cashier two hundred dollars to be changed into afghanis (the local currency), he went to the back room. After a long while he came back dragging a sack behind him. He opened the sack and pulled out bundle after bundle of 10,000 afghani notes and placed them on the counter. My 200 dollars were converted into 2 million afghanis. No wonder Khodaidad was so happy with the $100 tip that I had given him.

Since this pile of bills was too huge to carry, I bought a duffle bag at the gift shop, stuffed it with the afghanis, and asked Khodaidad to carry it up to our suite. Coming back down to the lobby, I ran into Noor Dilawari, the Afghan-American with a plan for Afghan's banking system who had arrived a couple of days before us. He told me about the 10:00 pm-to-dawn curfew and said that I should take care to be back in the hotel before then. Soon Afzal joined us and we went to the restaurant for high tea.

While we were in the restaurant I watched people start trickling in one after another. I knew most of them and was introduced to the others. Among those that I met was a beautiful young lady by the name of Mina Sherzoi, a cousin whom I had not met before. I was delighted to learn that she was the daughter of Rahim Sherzoi, the one who accompanied me to the failed meeting with Senator Frank Church's aide. Rahim soon arrived at the restaurant and joined us. We talked for hours about our good fortune to be back in the motherland and our plans for the future.

Every table in the dining hall was filled with Afghans from all walks of life and various parts of the world, with the majority from the

United States. After dinner I collected my Iridium Satellite telephone from my suite to make a call to Maribeth. Satellite phones were the only form of telecommunication in the country. Since there was no signal inside the hotel, I went out to the parking lot. As I was walking down the hill, the night guard came running to warn me that I should not stray too far from the hotel because the dogs roaming around the bottom of the hill had become accustomed to eating human flesh. Apparently, during the infighting between the different ethnic groups the bodies of the dead could not be picked up and became fodder for the hungry dogs of Kabul. I was shocked, to say the least, when I heard this news. I retracted my steps and walked around the parking lot looking for a strong satellite signal until I found one in front of the ballroom entrance door.

I dialed the United States and after two rings heard Maribeth's sweet voice. She had just returned from India. I told her about my trip and everything that had happened up to then, even the human-flesh-eating dogs. After hanging up, I made a mark on the spot where I had gotten the best satellite signal and then went up to our suite. Afzal was already sleeping. It had been a long day.

CHAPTER 17

THE PEOPLE'S PRINCE

The following morning, I was up bright and early and walked down to the dining room. It was not yet open for breakfast, so I walked out to the terrace to see the Bagh-e-Bala Palace, the residence of my great-grand father, King Abdurrahman. From afar, the palace looked the same, with its blue dome and towers. This had been the king's favorite residence. He spent most of the latter part of his life in Bagh-e-Bala until he died from gout in 1901.

Afzal and I had rented a van with a driver to take us on a tour of the city. The city of Kabul is divided into two regions separated by a mountain range and the Kabul River. On the one side are the city's wealthiest neighborhoods, Shar-e Now and Wazir Akbar Khan Mina, where most of the foreign embassies were located. This side also contains Macrorayan, a section of former Soviet-built residential apartment buildings. The Inter-Continental Hotel is located in the Karta Parwan neighborhood, and Kabul Polytechnic, an engineering college that had become the center of the Afghan Communist movement, was also in this area.

The Royal Palace, Lycée Esteqlal (French Academy), and my great-grandfather's mausoleum are also located on this side of the river.

The other side of the mountain contains neighborhoods called Karta Char, Karta She, and Kote Sangi, which are filled with residential and ministerial offices. This is also the section of the city that is home to Kabul University and most of the hospitals. Our family's two palaces, the Darul Aman and Tape Taj Beg, both designed by German architects, are also located in this region.

When we set out on our tour, my mind was imprinted with images of Kabul as I last saw it in 1978. I was in for a huge shock. Leaving the hotel and going through the city, past the Palace and the Mausoleum, we turned toward the Kabul River and headed towards the Kabul Zoo on the other side of the mountain. With my video camera running we went past the zoo, and looking through the viewfinder toward Karta Char Street I could not believe what I saw. Or better still . . . what I did not see. There was not one single building, house, or any other type of structure standing. Every piece of construction, every home was a pile of rubble.

At the intersection of Karta Char, the entire traffic police office complex was gone. We turned left on the once-majestic Darul Aman Avenue, and again there was nothing but rubble. This road, built during my uncle's reign, had been lined with huge birch trees. Now there were none to be found. We continued on to the end of the avenue to approach our family's two palaces, which had been built in the 1920s during my uncle King Amanullah's reign and connected by an underground tunnel. Slowing to a stop we found the Darul Aman Palace in ruins. Beyond it, the Tapa-e-Tajbeg Palace was also an unrecognizable heap of ruins.

Darul Aman had been built to house the king's administrative offices and as the formal venue where His Majesty would receive the public. In that bygone age the Palace was surrounded by formal gardens filled with multicolored roses and finely trimmed hedges like the grand royal gardens of France and Germany. Legend has it that when the foundation was dug, His Majesty buried a bag of gold under one of the pillars for good luck. The nearby Tapa-e-Tajbeg Palace was the Royal Family's residence.

The entire region was totally destroyed. Our driver told us that while the Soviets chopped down the ancient trees so the freedom fighters could not use them as cover, the rest of the destruction was not by the Soviets, but the warlords who waged war against one another and in so doing had destroyed more than fifty percent of the city. Our driver told us that most of the major fighting between the groups had taken place in that area.

I could not hold back my emotions. I burst out in tears when I saw what our own people had done to our beautiful city.

We headed north for about a ten-minute drive to Kabul University. The campus buildings were not badly damaged, but we learned that the underground rooms had been used for torturing and killing people. The dried blood on the floor had caked up and cracked.

On our way out of the campus area we saw a United Nations anti-mining group and stopped to ask them what they had observed. They told us that in every broken-down home that they examined, they found the water wells filled with dead bodies. In another instance, they had found a container filled with beheaded humans and mutilated women's bodies.

I could not mentally or emotionally absorb what I was seeing. Our family had served the nation for over two hundred years and had kept Afghanistan secure, its people united and independent. As a country we were poor, but free. We did not fight among ourselves, but had always united to fight against foreign enemies. Now we had become our own worst enemy. The majority of the fighting and killings were among the tribal groups from the North. No wonder the Taliban were received with open arms, I thought to myself.

As we continued to travel through the city we learned about more of the horrors of present-day Kabul. The driver told us that the city was divided among different ethnic groups and that individuals needed permission and documents to travel through the various areas. He described how one group had dug tunnels and travelled underground in order to avoid being caught, tortured, and killed. One of the vicious warlords they tried to evade, a man named Mazari, was known for his favorite pastime, the "dance of the dead man." Standing in front of a prisoner, he would signal for one of his soldiers to come from behind and with the swing of his sword remove the prisoner's head and immediately pour hot oil on his neck. The nervous system of the headless man would make his arms flail and his body rotate a few times before falling to the ground.

The driver went on to tell us that the same warlord had arrested him and another and had ordered them to be burned alive in a brick kiln.

While they were being taken to the place to be killed, another ethnic group appeared on the horizon and the guards fled, leaving them a few yards from the kiln. He said that that day Allah was looking out for him. He ran as fast as his legs would carry him.

The Taliban were no better. Leaving the city, we drove north through Afghanistan's grape and fruit country known as Shamali. Here the Taliban had not only set fire to every single building, but had also chopped down every fruit tree and cut up every grape vine, pouring acid on the remaining vines so that they would never grow again. As we were driving, I noticed red-painted rocks on either side of the road. Our driver was carefully staying away from the edge of the lane. When I asked him what the red rocks were for, he nervously told me, without taking his eyes off the road, that both sides of the road were mined and the red-painted rocks identified the locations of the mines. He advised us not to get out of the car to walk around or we would be blown up.

Keeping safely toward the center of the road we drove to Istalif, a resort built during the reign of my grandfather as a getaway residence from the city. Snuggled in a lush valley with crystal-clear mountain streams, Istalif was a favorite spot for our family's picnic outings. As we reached the "takht," the flat terrace where the palace was located, we saw that the centerpiece, the mansion, lay in rubble. We later learned that the Taliban had blown it up with dynamite.

Of all the areas they captured the Taliban had done the most damage in Shamali. Besides killing the residents, burning down the houses, and destroying the fields and orchards, they had also received the blessing of Mullah Omar to take any girls from the villages they plundered and marry them by force. As a result, a number of young girls had committed suicide.

Then our driver/tour guide took us to the brick kilns where he had escaped certain death. These objects were built of mud in the shape of a pyramid. They would make mud bricks and lay them down in layers against the inside wall of the kiln, fill the hollow space in the middle with firewood, and light it. The heat from the flames would bake the bricks.

As we drove away, our driver told us about another Taliban atrocity involving a man who was driving his expectant wife, who was in labor, to the hospital. The Taliban stopped his car, pulled out him and his wife, and threw the wife on the street. They gathered around her and waited for her to deliver. When the baby was born, they killed all three and left the bodies on the street.

I was sick to my stomach and asked the driver to stop the car. Braving the roadside mines, I jumped out before Afzal could stop me and threw up on the side of the road. I had heard and seen enough carnage. This was not my Afghanistan and these animals were not my people. These were not the same people who had defended their country against the multitudes of invaders and conquerors.

I decided then and there that I was going to do whatever I could—everything within my power—to help as many as I could.

On the way back to the hotel I asked the driver to take me to one of the newly opened music shops. I was surprised to see so many of these stores open for business, filled with everything from CDs to DVDs of Indian movies and all types of music systems and equipment. I purchased a Sony CD player and some lively Afghan music CDs for the hotel. I was intent on bringing sound and life back to that "dead" place.

As soon as I got to the hotel I made my way down to the electrical room to check out where to connect the CD player. Luckily, the Taliban had not destroyed the wiring system, so it was easy to hook up the sound system. As soon as everything was in place I slipped in the CD of the famous Afghan singer Ahmad Zahir, turned up the volume to the maximum, and ran upstairs to see the reaction of the guests and employees.

The lobby was full of amazed and sincerely happy faces. All of a sudden the hotel exploded with life, as guests streamed down from their rooms, employees filed in from every nook and cranny of the hotel, and even the outdoor security guards poured into the lobby and began dancing.

The manager could not find enough words to thank me. He told me that once again the Inter-Continental Hotel sounded like it did before the bloodshed destroyed the country.

All of this happiness reminded me of the Bamyan restaurant up on the fifth floor, my hangout of eons ago, so I walked over to the elevator to go up and take a look. The guard told me that the elevators had been broken for years and the parts could not be found in Kabul. I looked at the plaque on the inside of the elevator and saw that it was manufactured by OTIS. This was good news because Otis was located in my US "home" state of Connecticut. I noted the phone number on the plaque and went out to the spot in the parking lot where I could get a signal on my Iridium phone. I made the call and asked for the service department.

When I told the service man that the elevators in the hotel in which I was staying were not working and needed immediate attention, the service man was very cordial and asked me for the address of the hotel. I told him that it was the Inter-Continental Hotel in Kabul, Afghanistan . . . he hung up without a word. So much for Otis service. I expected them to at least tell me which neighboring country could provide the hotel with parts, but they did not take any further calls from me. Hopefully my future efforts to make improvements would be more successful.

That evening every one of the guests were gathered at the dining hall. Each table was occupied by a specific group of Afghans from the same country, the largest being the group of Afghan-Americans, followed by the Afghan-Germans. I knew most of these guests, so I went from table to table, greeting old friends. It was such a grand occasion. Each of us had returned home from different corners of the world and were ready to roll up our sleeves and help rebuild our battered homeland.

The Afghan-Americans had come to develop telecommunication, banking, and some engineering projects, and the Afghan-Germans had plans for the water purification and canalization systems. Still others were interested in mining and agriculture.

The waiters moved from table to table taking orders from the very limited menu of five items: grilled chicken, one type of white rice, a hamburger and French fries, spinach stew, and steak. Each one was a sorry excuse for food. I ordered the chicken and some French fries and was served a flattened piece of chicken breast that tasted like leather, soggy French fries, and stale tomatoes. Even though the food was bad, we ate it like a gourmet meal because we were so happy to re-forge our ties and talk about a new future for our home country.

Among the guests were my cousin, Dr. Zalmai Rassoul, Mina Sherzoi and her father Rahim Sherzoi (another cousin), former and current government ministers, businessmen, and others. Since curfew was at 10:00 pm, everyone stayed at the hotel and we talked until the wee hours in the morning.

After breakfast the next day I took my duffle bag of afghanis and got in my rented van to head for Chicken Street in Shar-e-Now. As soon as I stepped out of the van I was surrounded by a crowd of boys and girls begging for money. Among them were two beautiful girls who in a different country could have been child models. The one with the deep blue eyes, freckles, and light skin was called Saeeda. She was ten years old. The other, with slanting dark eyes and cute dimples on her cheeks and chin, was called Malalai, and she was eleven years old. All of these children were born during battle and had not known anything but hunger, poverty, and bloodshed. They all came from single-parent homes because their fathers were killed by the Taliban. Yet all fifteen of them were very well behaved and courteous.

Since it was lunch time, I asked them if they were hungry. With one voice they shouted yes. One of them added that they had not eaten since the day before. I then asked them if they would like to go and eat in a restaurant, and they gleefully agreed. So, like the Pied Piper I led them to the nearest restaurant, the good old Marco Polo, which, having been the only hamburger restaurant in town before The Twenty-Five Hour Club, was surprisingly still around.

When we got in, I asked the waiter to set a table for sixteen people and told the children to go wash their hands and faces. I ordered hamburgers, fries, and Pepsi for each of us, and when the boys and girls returned, their faces were clean and shining with their real beauty and good looks. I was amazed at how wonderful they looked. They sat down around the table, looking shy and uncomfortable. I told them to relax and enjoy the meal.

When the meal arrived and was placed in front of them, their behavior amazed me. Here they were, hungry, thirsty, and for the first time in their lives sitting in a restaurant—you would think that they would attack the food and gulp it down. No sir. They sat like well-behaved children, as if they had lived this life before. They were all looking at me to begin. I told them that they could go ahead and start eating. Even then, they each picked up their hamburgers gently and took small bites, followed by a French fry or two. They sipped their sodas and wiped their lips with the napkins they had placed on their laps. I fell in love with all of them.

During lunch each child gave me a glimpse of what he or she had gone through during the Taliban rule—how their fathers were dragged out and killed before their eyes and how they and their mothers were beaten with iron rods by the Taliban fighters. I just sat feeling guilty about the hell these innocent children had been through while I lived my comfortable life in the United States and Brazil. When we finished eating I asked each of them to come to me one at a time. I put the duffle bag in my lap and as each child came up I pulled out a wad of bills and, without counting how much, gave each one a bundle. The pure joy on their faces gave me a great deal of comfort.

Of the fifteen children, Saeeda and Malalai stood out. They appeared more mature and seemed to be in control of the others. They were the leaders.

Thereafter I made it a point to visit Chicken Street once a day to check on my brood. Malalai and Saeeda were there every day without fail. I asked them one day why they did not go to school, and they said if they did not beg on the streets their families would go hungry. They were the only providers for their mothers and siblings.

I decided that if I could save these two girls and their families, my trip to Afghanistan would be a success. I told Malalai and Saeeda that as of that day, they no longer needed to beg. I would get them enrolled in school and take care of all of their household expenses. I gave them money for clothes and then took them to a stationary shop and bought them everything they needed for school.

The next day I took Malalai and Saeeda to their school and told the principal that the girls were under my care and that she should report to me if there was any problem. I told her where I was living, and when I found out that she had not been paid for months, I went into my trusty duffle bag once again, gave her a bundle of afghanis, and told her that if she took care of my two kids, I would take care of her.

///////////

Over the next week I worked day and night with Afzal and our other partners to prepare our cell-phone system proposal for Abdul

Rahim, head of the Ministry of Communications. On the scheduled day of our visit, we gave a strong and detailed presentation. We knew that there were several other companies also bidding for the telephone project, including Alcatel of France who, we found out later, was making their presentation on behalf of Prince Agha Khan, the Leader of the Ismaeli Islamic sect.

In the meantime, the quality of food at the hotel had not improved, regardless of how much we complained. One day I got so fed up that I told the sixty-some guests that I was going to cook for them. I called the chef, gave him a list of ingredients that I needed, and then followed him to the kitchen. I should have waited to see the kitchen before opening my mouth about cooking.

The modern kitchen that I remembered was gone—the room was in total ruins. There was no oven to be found and not even a roof over our heads. The cook explained that the destruction had come from rockets launched from the outskirts of the city by the ruthless Gulbuddin Hekmatyar, founder of the Hezb-e Islami faction. All that was left of the kitchen facilities were two wooden burners held up by bricks, with two huge cooking pots on top. Now I knew why the chicken was so tough—they had nothing to cook it in. I did not know where or how they prepared it, and frankly I did not want to know.

In spite of the devastated conditions, I had made a promise to the guests and I was going to keep it. So when the groceries arrived, I went to the "kitchen" to start preparing a meal of saffron rice with chicken stew called *qorma chalow*.

I had never cooked meals on such burners and in such giant pots. One could place an entire sheep in one of those vessels. Nevertheless, with my pseudo-assistant chefs, I went to work. Unlike regular ovens in which one places the pot inside, with these traditional wood burners, when the rice is ready to be baked, they take most of the hot coal from underneath the pot and put it on top. This serves the same purpose of an electric or gas oven. When the dish was ready, I went out and made an announcement for all to gather in the dining room.

The food was served buffet style, and compared to what we had been eating, it was quite good. The guests were ecstatic about being served a home-made traditional dish and urged me many times after that to treat them again to my "culinary delights," which I was happy to do.

While Afzal and I were waiting for the Minister of Communication's response to our telecommunication proposal, I continued my tours of the city and the outskirts. As we once again drove near the remains of my royal ancestors' two palaces, which King Amanullah had built in the 1920s to commemorate Afghanistan's victory of independence over the British, they symbolized a nation that now lay in ruins. The destruction of these great palaces reminded me of the historical Balai Saar Fort, the former residence of Afghan kings that was occupied by the British on three different occasions. The British Ambassador allegedly committed suicide at the fort when he thought that the Afghans were attacking it. The story goes that he did not want to end up like Burns, the British commander who was killed at the fort during the first Anglo/Afghan war.

Situated on top of a steep hill, the fort was built over several centuries. There was a palace built on top, surrounded by high walls constructed with boulders, rocks, and mortar. Several high towers stood on these walls, manned by soldiers, and two deep wells were dug on the site to store potable water in the event of a siege. Down the hill, two more palaces and a number of private villas had been built. After the defeat of the British in the second Anglo/Afghan war (known as the battle of Maiwand, where the British allegedly lost an entire regiment), the British, under the command of General Roberts, came from India and attacked Balai Saar Fort. They razed the fort and its surrounding palaces and villas to the ground. General Roberts succeeded in removing any trace of the embarrassing failure of the British during the first Anglo/Afghan war.

My wandering thoughts brought tears to my eyes, thoughts of what was, what could have been, and what we had become. At that moment I cursed all the foreign countries and local groups who had played a role in the destruction of my motherland. Even though my heart ached for our beleaguered nation, the memory of these magnificent palaces gave me a deep sense of pride for being a nation that had defeated the British Empire not once, but three times. I said a silent prayer for the souls of the martyrs of the past and present before turning toward the road that would take me back to the hotel.

For the next two weeks I spent my time making contacts, renewing old friendships, and keeping a track of my brood on Chicken Street. I also met a great number of the US troops based in Kabul, who on several occasions invited me to visit with them at Camp Eggers, the US military base near the US Embassy. The soldiers dressed in civilian clothes and moved about the city mingling among the crowds without the slightest feeling of insecurity. The population at large welcomed them with affection and open arms.

One evening, Mina and I decided to throw a party at the hotel to celebrate our newfound nation. The 150-person guest list included all the guests of the hotel and several members of the US military. We hired a local band of musicians led by Momin Khan Beltoon, the legendary singer and virtuoso on the tanbur (the traditional long-necked string instrument). We held the function in one of the VIP rooms and, since alcohol was not available in Kabul, requested our foreign friends to bring the drinks. I prepared some of the food and instructed the hotel cooks on how to cook the rest. The music started with the tune for the attan, the Afghan national dance, in which everyone forms a circle and claps their hands as they move from side to side, much like the Jewish hora.

In the beginning the Afghan women were reluctant to join in the dance. I would hear none of it. I pulled each lady into the circle until every one of them was dancing gleefully. Our American guests were the next to be coaxed in, and although awkward at first, they soon mastered the art and danced their hearts out.

As the night went on, the party got more loud and joyful. Eventually, the women who were so shy about joining the circle were now dancing in groups, waving their slender arms and laughing and waving their long black hair. Guests were pouring bundles of afghani notes and dollars over the heads of the musicians, as was the custom. I just stood on the sidelines, in awe of what Mina and I had created.

The soldiers left soon after dinner to get back to camp by the 11:00 pm camp curfew. The rest of us continued well into the night. At around 3:00 am the exhausted hotel guests disappeared into the dark hallways of the hotel, heading for their rooms. Soon only Mina and I were left smiling and laughing at our success in bringing joy to Kabul. While we were talking, a serious-looking man walked up to us and in a stern voice asked us if we knew what day it was. We told him, still smiling, that it was a day of joy and freedom and asked him who he was.

He introduced himself as an intelligence officer responsible for the hotel's activities. We congratulated him for his position and asked him if he had enjoyed the evening. He was not amused. In a grave tone, he told us that the day represented Maulood-e-Sharif. We said that we *were* celebrating the Prophet's (PBUH) birthday. Without acknowledging our comment, he went on to tell us that that was the day that the Prophet (PBUH) had gone to heaven. Oops. We were silent. We had both been out of Afghanistan so long that we had forgotten the meanings of some of the religious days.

We apologized but also insisted that we were sure that we would be forgiven for our misunderstanding, as we were celebrating the freedom of our motherland and the cessation of the bloodbath that had befallen our nation for several decades. We said good night to him and left to go to our respective rooms. We thought we had heard the last of it, but the next day we were told that word had gotten to President Karzai and he was not very happy. He accepted the fact, however, that we deserved the right to celebrate.

After breaking the partying ice that night many people starting hosting parties within and outside of the hotel. One evening a group of us was invited to a party in the home of a man named Hashmat Ghani who lived in the affluent of Wazir Akbar Khan Mina section of the city. We piled up in my rented Taurus van and drove to his house. The evening was wonderful, but watchful of the citywide 10:00 pm curfew, we kept checking our watches. Since the party started warming up at about 10:00 pm, Hashmat called one of his friends in the security department to get the night code. This code was used if stopped by the military while travelling on the roads beyond the curfew hour. The system included a code and a counter code; for example, if the code was "Day," the counter code would be "Night."

Feeling comfortable about this arrangement, we continued to party until well beyond midnight. Since I had sent my driver back to the hotel well before the curfew, Hashmat offered his driver to return us in his van. I sat in front with the driver while the others piled into the two rows of seats behind us.

When we arrived at the first check point near the Iranian Embassy, a soldier jumped in front of the van, pointed a machine gun directly at us, and yelled "HALT!" Another soldier came to the driver's side and poked his head in and asked for the code. Our driver, whom I assumed had joined in the party and had a few drinks, started joking with the soldier by telling him that he had forgotten the password code. He said that he had been driving all day and everyone was tired.

The soldier was getting angry and the one with the machine gun was growing fidgety, moving his weapon from side to side and up and down. Angrily, I told the driver to stop the jokes and tell the soldier the password code.

In a whisper, the driver did as I ordered. The soldier responded with the counter. The rule was that once the counter was relayed, the one by the car had to yell "Safe!" to the one with the weapon, at which time he would lower his weapon and let the vehicle pass. But instead of doing that, the soldier by the window asked our driver to bring him a pack of cigarettes on his way back. The driver agreed and drove off with speed. The armed soldier opened fire and we heard the thud-thud-thud of bullets hitting the back of the van. Fortunately, none of the bullets entered the car, or someone would have been dead by the way we were packed in.

The driver put the foot to the pedal and flew like the wind to the next intersection. Even before we got to that point I saw a row of machine gun-mounted vehicles facing toward us. We came to a screeching halt. A well-dressed officer came to my window, greeted me, and asked where we were going. I introduced myself and told him that my guests and I were on our way to the Inter-Continental Hotel. Even though he recognized me, he apologetically informed me that because of what happened at the last stop the Ministry of Defense was sending an investigation team to check out what was going on.

After about half an hour of waiting, a car arrived with a military officer on board. He recognized me and greeted me politely and advised me about the dangers of running through the check points. He said that the soldier at the last gate was a rookie and a bad shot. Had it been one of the professional soldiers, we would have ended up with a number of casualties.

He ordered the soldiers to disperse, thus allowing our vehicle to continue our late-night trip to the hotel.

///////////

Among the tribal people who came to see me during my stay in Kabul in early 2002 was a young man named Omar. His father was the tribal chief of a district called Jaghatoo in the Province of Ghazni. (In 2013 UNESCO declared Ghazni the Asian Capital of Islamic Culture.) Omar came to the hotel and asked me if the Americans would be willing to help rebuild some of the schools in the Jaghatoo District. I submitted his request to the colonel at Camp Eggers and he eagerly accepted to arrange a group of engineers to visit Jaghatoo.

On the appointed date, I arrived at Camp Eggers at 6.00 am, accompanied by a young Afghan-American woman, Seema, who had come to Afghanistan from New York. The colonel was waiting for us. I agreed to lead the convoy of three Humvees manned by twelve soldiers, four structural engineers, and driven by three female marines.

We left Kabul and headed for Jaghatoo via the Kabul-Kandahar highway, a sorry excuse for a road or what was left of it. They called it a highway, but I named it the "gutterway." Every inch of the road was covered with deep holes, so much so that our vehicles could only travel at 15 to 25 miles per hour. As we travelled through the villages, my van and the Humvees must have made a curious site, for groups of villagers came out to greet us as we rolled by.

Before reaching the village of Maidan Shar, the bottom of my van hit a rock, embedded in one of the deep holes and we heard a crunching sound. The driver stopped the van on the side of the road and went out to check the problem. He looked under the van and came up with a worried look on his face. He told me that the rock had cracked the oil pan and we were leaking oil. Since we were close to the village, we drove as fast as the road condition would allow and came to a stop in the middle of the town's shopping center. The Humvees came to a stop behind us. While I went to tell the colonel about my predicament, my driver walked toward the stores to find a mechanic.

A large group of villagers surrounded our vehicles. The U.S. security guards were sitting on top of their Humvees, keeping an eye on our surroundings. Omar stepped over to talk to some of the elders standing among the sightseers. Apparently, he told them who I was, for within minutes several men with long white beards walked up to me with wide grins on their faces. One by one they threw their arms around me, greeted me in the Afghan fashion, and kept repeating the name of Allah and thanking Him for bringing me back to the country.

They told me that their people supported my uncle, King Amanullah, during the insurgency of 1929.

After our warm greetings the men asked how they could help. I told them that my van needed repairs, and they immediately summoned one of the men standing in the group and ordered him to take care of the van. They then whispered something to another man who then ran to one of the buildings near the road. Soon a garage door opened and a white car rolled out. The man drove over to me and handed me the keys. The elders told me that their driver would take me to my destination while the mechanic fixed the damage to my van. My driver could then meet up with us in Jaghatoo.

The American soldiers were standing around taking pictures and videos of the gathering, and a number of them were sipping on cups of tea. The young Afghan men were totally amazed to see young blond women in military fatigues. They rushed away and returned with flowers to offer to them.

Finally, after many hugs and handshakes, we were once again on our way. Several miles out of Maidan Shar, Omar directed the driver to drive through the open grounds to the right of the highway. The driver did as instructed, and we began driving through a hard, desert-like terrain, followed by my entourage of Humvees. After several miles of flat ground, we reached a hilly area. At that point, my car blew a tire. Once again, we all stopped, and my driver got out to change the tire. A few minutes later we started up a winding route, up and around several hills. Once we were clear of the hills, we once came to flat ground.

As we were driving, I saw a bus in the far-off distance with a group of people sitting on top of it. As the bus got closer, it began to slow down. So did we. When we reached each other, the group from the top of the bus hastily climbed down and came toward us. To tell the truth, I was concerned, for we were in the middle of nowhere and surrounded by hills. If these people meant us harm, we were in trouble.

I slowly pulled my pistol out of my belt and put it under my thigh. My Afghan-American friend, Hasina, saw this and got a worried look on her face. I looked in the rear-view mirror and saw the soldier on top of the Humvee move behind the gun on the turret.

As it turned out, we had nothing to fear. The men had scrambled down to greet us in the most traditional Afghan way. They formed a circle around two men with large skin drums hanging around their necks. As soon as the drummers started to play, the men went into a frenzy, dancing the attan. They turned from side to side and twirled up into the air, waving their long hair.

My fellow travelers asked what was happening. When I explained that they were the welcoming committee, they were amazed. They pulled out their cameras and videos and started documenting this unbelievable gesture on their behalf. The group continued to dance for well over an hour until I raised my hand and requested them to stop. I told them that we were running late and had to get to Jaghatoo. The dancers shook the hands of the Americans and started to climb back on the bus, which was on its way to Ghazni. When the marines started to board their vehicles, I noticed that two of them, a male and female marine, were sitting among the dancers on the top of the bus. I called out to them to find out what they thought they were doing. They smiled and yelled back that they would follow us on the bus to Jaghatoo. I laughed out loud. They were so overtaken by the hospitality and friendliness of the people and felt so safe and comfortable among them that they did not ask anyone where the bus was headed. I yelled back that the bus was going in the opposite direction to Ghazni. They looked disappointed and reluctantly slid off the side of the bus, aided by the helping hands of their new friends.

Once again we were on our way. When we neared the village of Jaghatoo I heard the familiar sound of the drums. The closer we got, the louder the sounds. As we turned the corner toward the village, I was astonished at the sight. The villagers had erected tall gates covered with Afghan and American flags and surrounded with flowers. The villagers were standing in two lines along each side of the dirt road, clapping and yelling welcome as we drove through.

When we got to the first decorated gate I noticed a group of white-bearded elders. We stopped and I got out of my car just as the colonel was getting out of his Humvee. We both walked over to the old men and I started greeting each in the traditional Afghan embrace, while the colonel shook their hands. Then a couple of Afghan girls brought bouquets of flowers and handed them to us.

We then greeted the crowds who were gathering around us, and a few minutes later the village elder gave a welcoming speech. When he was finished, it was my turn to talk. I thanked the gathering and told tham that it was an honor to once againb be among the very people who had stoo by my Uncle, King Amanullah, during the 1929 uprising. That I had come to Jaghatoo with our American friends to help in rebuilding the schools that the Taliban and Al Qaeda had destroyed. When I was speaking the Chief Elder asked us to accompany him to the clinic in the village center. We walked with him, followed by the marines and a female military nurse. The villagers followed. Before coming to Jaghatoo I had sent message to the elders stating that I did not want to see a single gun in the area, and none was visible. Everything expressed an atmosphere of friendship.

We walked through the clinic which was devoid of any medical equipment or furniture. One cabinet against the wall contained a few boxes of medicine. The head medical specialist looked almost embarrassed at the bareness of the clinic. The marine nurse went back to her vehicle and came back with several boxes of medical necessities including syringes, bandages, antibiotics, and other items that were accepted with deep gratitude. The colonel promised that once he got back to Kabul he would make sure to send more supplies.

We then went on a tour of the schools that were destroyed by the Taliban and Al Qaeda. When we got there, we were greeted by groups of students, boys and girls, standing in two lines, some carrying the Afghan flag and others holding up pictures of King Amanaullah. As we got out of our vehicles, the children all chanted "Hooray!" and started clapping and wishing us welcome. A couple of young girls brought us flowers. I was bursting with pride. How wonderful it was to be back home. To be back among my people who still remembered us with deep affection and respect. After the greeting ceremony, we walked up to the schools. Rubble was strewn around where the schools once stood, and all the students were seated on the bare ground. The blackboard was a piece of shredded plywood painted black. For chalk, the teacher used rock lime.

The U.S. Marines were moved by the dedication of the teachers who had not received any salary, and also to the commitment of the students, both boys and girls, to getting an education. Wherever we went, we were surrounded by young children who greeted us with huge grins. Looking at them, one could not believe the dire circumstances in which they had lived and survived.

After visiting the bombed-out skeletons of the schools we were led to a beautiful rose garden with fresh clear waters flowing in small streams around a wide-open space. The space was covered with carpets. *Toshak* and *balesht*—seating mattresses and huge pillows—were laid out in an L shape on the outer edge of the carpets, and in front of these bowls of fruit and platters of nan were placed on traditional tablecloths, or *destarkhan.*

We were guided to sit on the cushions at the short section of the L, while the others took their places along the long side. As soon as we sat down and leaned against the comfortable pillows, young men appeared carrying water containers, basins, and towels.

The colonel looked at me quizzically. I told him that it was customary in Afghanistan for everyone to wash their hands before partaking of food. The colonel announced this to the rest of the marines. Looking around, I was surprised to see all the marines squatting Afghan style next to their Afghan hosts, with their guns out of sight. This was a great honor to the hosts, as the US military always left guards near their vehicles, and these soldiers never joined in an event such as this but kept to their military rations. I was deeply pleased that they apparently felt very welcomed and safe among their hosts.

The villagers had not spared anything in serving us the most varied and sumptuous meal I had ever experienced. The platters and bowls were filled with a dozen different types of stews, several barbequed whole lambs known as *Qauw*, spiced basmati and other types of rice, and many varieties of kebobs including lamb and chicken.

Our American friends were overwhelmed. They took pictures and videos of the entire set up. They also ate with their hands like their Afghan hosts, and it was funny to see them picking up a handful of rice covered with stews and trying to deliver the handful to their mouths, spilling almost half on their uniforms. The art of eating with one's hand is learned over many years. The objective is to pick up the rice with four fingers and the thumb and then once in front of the mouth, push the food into the mouth with the thumb. I gave my friends a crash course in "Eating by Hand 101." I was amazed on how quickly they picked up the art and by the end of the meal, they all had become experts.

They ate so much that it made me concerned about them getting sick.

It is customary in Afghanistan that after a good meal the guests must burp to show that they have enjoyed the food. When our hosts started burping, again the colonel looked at me with curiously. I smiled and told him and the other marines about the custom. No sooner had I finished my sentence than every one of marines started burping, including the two women.

Soon after we finished the feast a group of young men began to clear the food while another group started laying down desserts and fruits. The dessert was made from milk and sugar. As a caution, since the milk may have been out for a while, I recommended that the marines concentrate on the fruits. After dessert, we were served green and black tea accompanied with various types of sweets and chocolates.

It was getting late in the day and I thanked the tribal elder for his great hospitality. I told him that the Americans would never forget their experience in Jaghatoo. The colonel verified my statement and we began the long process of bidding our hosts farewell.

The whole entourage of more than fifty individuals stood in one line, and I went first to embrace the elders and then shake the hands of the others. The marines followed suit. After everyone had said their goodbyes, a group of five very handsome young men coyly asked me if the beautiful American lady, referring to the blue-eyed marine driver, would accept any one of the five as her husband. When I translated their request to her, at first she blushed. Then she smiled and stretched out her hand to each of the five and told them that had she not had a husband waiting for her in the USA she would have gladly selected one of them for a husband. Now it was the young men's time to blush. Against tribal culture, she hugged each of them. No one minded her friendly gesture.

Saying goodbye, we all piled up in our cars and left for Kabul. By this time my car was repaired and in good condition to make the journey back.

//////////

After clearing the hilly dirt roads, we finally made it to the main road to Kabul. As I led the caravan of vehicles over the pot-holed highway I kept a close eye on the Humvees close behind. At one point the gap between us grew larger and I told my driver to stop. For some reason the Humvees had stopped, and I got out to see what the problem was.

All the marines were out of their vehicles and gathered around the first Humvee. The vehicle had hit a large, deep pothole and broken the axle. I recommended leaving the Humvee behind and loading up the passengers in my van and the remaining Humvees. The colonel thought that that was a good idea, but he had to clear it with his headquarters first.

After making radio contact, his request was rejected and he was ordered to stay put with the vehicles and his team until help arrived from Kabul. The time was now close to 7:00 pm and it was getting dark. I could not stay with them as I was not part of the military and I had to get back to my hotel before the 10:00 pm curfew.

While I was talking to the colonel the marines were unloading their military food packages and dumping them on the desert ground. My driver and Omar gathered armfuls of the packages and loaded them into the back of the van. They could not believe that the Americans were throwing away all this food.

I said goodbye to the colonel and the soldiers and left with deep concern for their safety. Although the reception extended by my countrymen throughout our day-long journey was extremely hospitable, I could not guarantee the actions of others.

When we reached the village where my van had broken down I sent Omar to seek out the village elder. They soon returned and I told the elder about the caravan's breakdown and asked him to keep an eye out for any trouble. I also asked him to assist the marines if necessary. He promised to do that and to send a group of his fighters to the vicinity to keep watch. I told him to keep his people far enough away so as not to be mistaken as enemies by the Americans. I thanked him and we drove off into the dark night.

My driver was doing an excellent job in weaving the van around the craters on the road. But the pace was slow and I was getting very concerned about the approaching curfew.

In the distance, in the dim light of the headlights, I saw a log lying across the road. I told the driver to slow down and I became very concerned. Thinking that the log may be the work of highway thieves, I unholstered my pistol and grabbed the driver's Kalashnikov. I took the safety off and told the driver to approach the log slowly. Deep ravines on either side of the road prevented us from driving around it, so slowly, very slowly, we approached the log.

While I was considering how to move the log off the road, an armed uniformed soldier appeared out of the darkness. Breathing a sigh of relief that it was not a bandit, I told the driver to stop. Just to be safe, I had my finger on the trigger of the machine gun.

The soldier approached the open window with his weapon pointed toward us. When he reached the van, still pointing the weapon, he asked us who we were, where we had come from, and where we were going. He poked his head inside and when he saw a female among the passengers, he relaxed and drew down his weapon.

When my driver told the soldier who I was, he immediately saluted me and apologetically told me that it was very dangerous to be out driving at night, as the highway was infested with thieves who killed travelers like us for money and the vehicle. He told us that we should not go any further, but instead spend the night at their camp.

I thanked the soldier for his concern and advice, but explained that we could not stay overnight because people were waiting for us in Kabul and they would be very concerned if we did not show up. Also, I added, we had to take the young lady back to her house before the curfew. I glanced at Seema, who was as calm as she had been throughout all the events of the day. I was amazed that she seemed to be enjoying the whole experience.

By now the soldier was joined by several others, five in total, and all brandishing the familiar Kalashnikovs. They all insisted that we should not go any farther, but I respectfully refused. I thanked them and told the driver to drive on. Before raising the gate to let us through, the soldiers told us not to stop if we came across any log barricade across the road, but to go around it, and if we could not get past it, to turn around and come back to their camp.

I thanked them, and as a gesture of gratitude for their concern gave each of them $100.00. At first they refused, but I insisted. I knew how little they were paid and $100.00 would go a long way to help their families. They were delighted to receive my gift and fared us well.

We drove off into dark, bouncing over every hole on the road. I clutched the machine gun in my lap and glanced in every direction for signs of danger, but it was of no use. The night was so dark that the only visible area was the patch of road lit up by our headlights.

After a while on the road, I noticed headlights in the far-off distance heading our way. Fearing the worst, I told the driver to pull off the road and park with the lights off and the engine running. My plan was simple: we would wait until the vehicle got close to us, and as it passed us we would speed out without turning on our lights and head toward Kabul as fast as the van could travel.

When the headlights got closer, I noticed that there were two sets. This made me more alarmed, but as I contemplated what to do the vehicles went by us and I noticed the familiar shape of the US military Humvees. They were apparently on their way to assist the other marines that we had left behind. To say that I was relieved would be an understatement. We all laughed at our situation and pulled out of our so-called hiding place and back onto the gutted, sorry excuse for a highway.

Without any further delay or incident, we reached the outskirts of Kabul. We could see what little lights were operational, blinking in the distance and noted that we had about 45 minutes before the curfew.

When we reached the city, we drove straight to Seema's house, and after dropping her off headed to the Inter-Continental Hotel. On the way, the driver and Omar started arguing about how to divide the military food packets between themselves. They dropped me off with 15 minutes to spare and I could hear them arguing about the food trays as they pulled off.

I quietly walked up to my room by the back stairs so as not to wake anyone on the floors, since my cousin Afzal and our partners had an appointment with the Communication Minister Rahim in the morning. He had promised us an office space in the ministry headquarters, which were in a 16-story building, the only high-rise structure in the city at the time.

I was still too excited about the events of the day to fall asleep. I went out on the terrace and looked over the sparsely lit city and my thoughts once again went back to the wonderful times that I had spent in this hotel. The many tennis games I played with friends and relatives. The night I put on a fashion show around the swimming pool, where young ladies of many nationalities modeled dresses I had designed for the occasion.

Then I thought of the hospitality that my people in Jaghatoo had bestowed upon my American guests and men this day. I knew I would never forget their utter joy of seeing a member of our family in the same area where my uncle, King Amanullah Khan, had bid farewell to his supporters and his beloved Afghanistan in 1929 before leaving the country, or the sounds of the drums and the dancers and delicious and sumptuous meal served. It was truly an eventful day.

Standing there on the terrace, the best years of my life passed before my eyes. The past eight years felt like an entire lifetime and filled my heart with both sadness and joy. Tears rolled down my cheeks as I remembered what I had lost. What my family had lost and my beloved Afghanistan had lost. Yet I also felt a sense of joy for having had the opportunity to return to my homeland.

Allowing the joy to overcome my sorrow, I buried the anguish deep in my heart, wiped my tears, said a silent prayer, and closed the chapter of the past. I turned my thoughts toward a new chapter for my beleaguered nation's future and vowed to play a positive part in it.

A warm embrace of the night enveloped me, as if to tell me that the nation was elated that the prodigal son had returned to the land of his forefathers. Satisfied, I went to bed and immediately fell asleep, dreaming of a new beginning both for Afghanistan, and me.

ABOUT THE AUTHOR

Prince Ali Seraj of Afghanistan is the founder of the Prince Ali Seraj Institute for Peace and Reconstruction (www.pasi.one). Born in Kabul, Afghanistan, he is the descendant of twelve generations of Afghan kings. Seraj attended the University of Connecticut and holds dual U.S./Afghan citizenship. He is a sought-after speaker on Afghanistan and serves as an independent consultant on policy matters to government officials and organizations.